I0458780

PRINCESSES, UNICORNS, AND SUPERHEROES

A PRESCHOOL OWNER'S MAGICAL JOURNEY

BY

Ashli Karaman

The moral rights of the author have been asserted

All rights reserved

No part of this publication maybe reproduced, stored in a retrieval system or transmitted in any form or by any means, without the prior permission in writing of the publisher or the author, nor be otherwise circulated in any form of binding or cover other than that in which it is published and without a similar condition including this condition being imposed on the subsequent purchaser.

The Empire Publishers publishing
12808 West Airport Blvd Suite 270M Sugar Land, TX 77478

https://empirepublishers.co/about-us

Our books may be purchased in bulk for promotional, educational, or business use.
Please contact The Empire Publishers at +(844) 636-4576, or by email at support@theempirepublishers.com

First Edition 2025

Dedication

To my husband, my rock, who stood steadfastly by my side: your absolute support was the quiet strength that allowed this journey to unfold. Thank you for always having my back.

To my father, whose belief in my dreams was a constant guiding light: thank you for planting the seeds of possibility and nurturing my aspirations.

To my brother and mom, for your constant presence, your listening ears, and the comforting knowledge that you were always there: thank you for being my enduring foundation.

And finally, to my children, my brightest stars: you were the spark, the inspiration, the tiny, magical beings who showed me the boundless wonder of your world and inspired me to be so much more than I ever imagined. This story, in its own whimsical way, is for you.

Message From the Author

As you take the journey through these pages with me, you will hear these stories through my "I," my perspective as the preschool owner. But the heart and soul of these tales, the moments of wonder, the triumphs, and even the occasional tantrum, truly belong to the incredible teachers who were in the classrooms each and every day. These are mostly their frontline stories that I was lucky to be a part of.

Teachers are the ones on the front lines. The magical beings who love, nurture, guide, and inspire your little ones. I had the privilege of witnessing their dedication from my position as preschool owner, and it is their stories, their daily acts of kindness, their creative solutions, and their unwavering passion that I've had the honor of retelling here.

Thank you to all the early childhood educators who make the magic happen. This book is as much yours as it is mine.

Table of Contents

Chapter 1: The Accidental Entrepreneur

O kay, let's be honest. I never woke up one morning and thought, "You know what? I'm going to run a preschool empire!" It was more like, "Hmmm... I have young kids. I was an elementary school teacher before. I graduated with a business degree. How hard can running my own business be?" I mean, how different could 4-year-olds be from 4th graders I taught? Famous last words, right?

It all started with me looking for a school for my young kids. When I came home yet again frustrated with how few good preschool options there were, I looked at my kids and thought, "There has to be something better than this."

One school had a waiting list so long I might as well have applied when I was pregnant (which later on I found out they, in fact, do!). Another had teachers yelling down the hallway, and I could feel my stomach twist in that uncomfortable, "nope, not this one either" way. The final straw was the place that locked the front door during tours and had TVs on in every room—blaring cartoons while toddlers sat zombified during what was described as "movie day."

I remember venting to my husband and my parents, trying to make sense of it. I had three young boys—Preston,

Pierce, and Parker—and I just knew we could do better for my kids. And for all other kids who deserved better!

"Well," my mom said, half-joking, "You've always loved kids, and you're not afraid to organize a bit of chaos. Why don't you open a school yourself?"

I laughed. "I'd need a building, teachers, licenses… a miracle!"

But the idea stuck.

Within a few weeks, I was filling out forms for an SBA loan with trembling hands. I didn't know how to open a school or start a business. I just knew that if I was going to trust someone with my child, I wanted it to feel like a second home. So, I decided to create that home myself. At the time, I was balancing my corporate career in oil and gas while raising my three boys—Preston, Pierce, and Parker. When my youngest was just shy of a year old, I started thinking about what kind of environment I wanted for him. A place where he could learn, explore, and be surrounded by warmth and curiosity. That simple thought—just a mother wanting the best for her child—became the spark that ignited my journey into early childhood education.

My first "class" didn't start because I dreamed of running a school—it started because the preschool search for my own sons was downright appalling. I remember touring one facility where the director proudly told me, "We don't believe in outdoor play." Meanwhile, there was a faint smell of bleach and despair lingering in the air, and a toddler gnawing on a plastic block like it was jerky. I walked out of there and immediately called my mom.

"Maybe I'll just keep him home with me for a while," I said.

My mother, ever the realist (and a woman who raised two kids herself), laughed and said, "That's cute. Just remember, kids thrive with other kids. They need socialization and friends! Not to mention your boys have so much energy and curiosity; they would love learning, doing experiments, and playing outside!"

She wasn't wrong.

But the deeper I got into the search, the clearer it became—if I wanted my children to have the kind of early learning experience I imagined, the kind filled with joy, play, exploration, and real connections, I might just have to build it myself. (Spoiler: Very.)

Fast forward a couple of months, and my life was busy with info meetings and engulfed with loan paperwork. During one of my info meetings, that's when the big, scary, thrilling leap happened—a husband and wife handed me a check for their son's registration fee. Whoa! Now I had officially enrolled my first student at my school that was still under construction. It just became real. I was awe-struck by the incredible responsibility bestowed on me by these future parents and promised myself I would do everything I could to fulfill all their expectations.

Finding future parents was easier than finding the money to fund this dream. And that's where the real leap began—figuring out how to pay for it all. I remember sitting in a bank office with my father, signing paperwork for the loan that would fund this dream. Before we ended up signing paperwork in the banker's office, it all started at lunch. You see, when I shared my dreams and goals with my dad, he contacted a bank loan officer he knew. Lance, the banker, was willing to give me a chance because of my dad's high praises over lunch. Over a plate of fish and chips, I poured out my heart – and my entire business plan – to Lance. I'm talking grand ideas, future money-making predictions, and every demographic detail you could imagine. And let me tell you, for my first-ever business pitch, I was *uber* prepared. So prepared, in fact, that I slid my meticulously organized business plan binder across the table right alongside the ketchup. The resulting stain on my suit? Totally irrelevant. Lance saw past the spilled condiment and straight into my numbers, my research, and most importantly, my burning passion. A couple of weeks later, we were officially drowning in loan paperwork – a true sign of progress!

The day of the loan signing, my hands were literally shaking. It was terrifying. I wasn't just opening a school—I was signing up for property decisions, plumbing delays, and more financial responsibility than I'd ever carried. But it was also exhilarating. I could see it in my head: bright classrooms filled with joyful chaos, a cozy reading corner, a playground echoing with laughter. And I had one of my biggest supporters right next to me: my father!

The property we chose was nestled right near the master-planned neighborhood where we lived—which meant my house was nearby, my kids were already locked in friendly neighborhood sports rivalries, and most importantly, I knew the area like the back of my hand. I *was* one of the parents we were hoping to serve! And if there's one thing I've learned in business, it's that location isn't just a line on a map—it's a key ingredient to success.

In a short amount of time, I was busy finalizing furniture orders, evaluating paint samples, hiring teachers and directors, while at the same time handling full-blown construction: blueprints, contractors, permits, inspections— the works. Oh, and yes, meeting with future parents, enrolling our future students, and managing crib waitlists! It was all a whirlwind. So exciting!

The whole process was a crash course in entrepreneurship. I was choosing flooring one day and meeting with city inspectors the next. I learned the difference between fire code and building code and how to explain your vision to a construction crew who had zero interest in pastel wall paint.

It wasn't easy—but every foundation poured, every wall raised, brought me one step closer to building something real, something lasting. A place where kids could learn, play, grow- and where a dream was turning into reality, one nail at a time.

The school was still very much under construction— drywall dust in the air, paint samples everywhere, and my ever-so-ambitious timeline estimating we were "just two months away" from opening. (Spoiler: wildly optimistic.) It was time to start hiring. First on my list? My Director. My ride-or-die. The peanut butter to my jelly. Mickey to my Minnie. Tom to my Jerry. You get the idea—I needed *my person.*

So, I tossed my hopes and a job ad into the digital universe (yep, good ol' Craigslist), and soon found myself swimming in about fifty resumes. Let's just say… reviewing them was an emotional journey. I had everything from a university professor with more degrees than classroom time, to a high school senior who confidently declared she was "great with kids." My dream Director was someone who could juggle teachers like a seasoned ringmaster, smother kids in love like a favorite aunt, and charm parents like they were all neighbors from way back. Simple ask, right? Wrong. So wrong.

After a long stretch of cringe-worthy interviews (including one woman who asked how much she'd have to "deal with *those* kids"—yes, really), a resume caught my eye. Jackie. She was moving from out of state, had been a principal, and her accolades were practically glowing. We Skyped (throwback!), and I was dazzled. Her credentials sparkled like gold. Sure, there was a teensy "I'm-better-than-this" energy lurking beneath her words, but I ignored it. Because wow—that *resume.* I was convinced I'd found my Jelly.

But just to be thorough (and maybe out of loyalty to my organized calendar), I went ahead with my last few interviews. And then—bam—there was Annie. She hadn't been a director yet, but she was the long-time assistant director stuck behind a glass ceiling. She was warm, whip-smart, hilarious, and radiated this raw hunger to make a difference. After her interview, my gut was practically staging a protest march for Team Annie... but

I chose Jackie anyway. Because, well, qualifications.

Big mistake. HUGE.

Jackie, as it turned out, was *exactly* what my gut had warned me about—brilliant on paper, but a poor fit in the heart of our school. Two months in, I politely showed her the exit. And then? I called Annie.

Hiring Annie was like flipping on the lights. She became our glue, our spark, and stayed for over a decade of joy, growth, and glitter-filled adventures. That's when I truly learned: paper doesn't hold the magic—people do. And when someone shows up with heart, hustle, and the right vibe? That's the person you bet on. Every single time.

However, when you're building a business from scratch, apparently the universe decides to throw everything *but* the kitchen sink at you. And sometimes, it throws a kitchen sink full of snow, just to keep things interesting. You'll hit delays, deadlines will stretch like a toddler's patience, things will be on backorder (because, of course), and then there are those delightful weather surprises – think hurricanes, but also, bizarrely, snow.

So, for context, picture this: we live where summer is basically a giant oven, and winter means you might, *maybe*, need a light sweater. Construction on our building was finally, gloriously, done. Like, *finished*. And wouldn't you know it, on the second-to-last workday of December, we got our shiny Certificate of Occupancy from the fire marshal. Woo-hooo! Victory dance ensued! Naturally, the very next day, the absolute last workday of December, I practically skipped to the childcare license office, Certificate of Occupancy and Childcare License Application clutched in my hand, ready to cross that finish line. And what did I find? A "CLOSED DUE TO SNOW" sign. Snow! In this climate, it literally *never* snows, except, apparently, on the one day I desperately needed to get my license application turned in. That utterly impossible, inconvenient snowfall pushed our grand opening back a couple of weeks, right into the dreaded post-holiday slump. You just can't make this stuff up!

***

I always envisioned a serene, play-based learning environment—where kids were free to explore and learn as a byproduct of having fun! It was the closest thing to how we grew up—schools full of adventure, friends, and learning opportunities, uninterrupted by devices. The teachers at my not-yet-built school would play games with them on the playground, the same ones we played as kids, and do fun science experiments together!

Word spread, and what started as a small idea quickly gained traction. People started asking and posting about the "new school" coming up through construction. I began hosting information meetings to talk about my school that was under construction. During these meetings, I was able to give interested future parents information about our play-based curriculum, introduce myself and my background, and, as the date inched closer to opening, introduce some of our team members as well. It was exciting that they wanted to be a part of this new vision! Running a preschool taught me that toddlers can form alliances stronger than any political treaty—until someone takes the last cracker. That a day without a spill is a miracle. That early childhood educators are superheroes in disguise.

I imagined soft music playing, children happily engaged in activities, and sunlight streaming in just so. I even bought one of those fancy wooden toy sets that promised to boost cognitive development. In my mind, it was going to be magical.

Reality, however, had other plans. The first day of my school opening went something more like this: Liam—a tiny tornado in a superhero cape—was determined to "rescue" every toy from its rightful place. Lily could turn any space into a disaster zone in under 60 seconds. Aiden just asked "why" questions all day. Max would sit quietly for an hour, then suddenly let out a roar that could wake the dead. And Emily? She loved glitter. So. Much. Glitter.

Within the first five minutes, I had a superhero-themed dinosaur rampage, a kinetic sand situation, and a crying fit over a broken crayon. I thought I stepped on something sharp—only to realize it was googly eyes. That's right. Even the craft supplies were judging me.

I looked around at the absolute chaos and thought, "What have I done?"

But then something magical happened. Liam, mid-rampage, suddenly stopped and started building an elaborate dinosaur fortress. He was so focused, so engaged, that I couldn't help but smile. And when he proudly showed me his creation, his face lit up like a Christmas tree.

That's when it hit me—this wasn't just "babysitting" or "caregiving." This was something special.

And oh, their stories...

Like the time little Sophia brought in an earthworm and insisted it was her new pet. "Look, Ms. Ashli! He's my friend!" she announced, holding it way too close to my face.

Cue instant chaos—half the kids screamed, half were fascinated, and one tried to put it in their pocket. (Wiggles the Worm was eventually released back into the wild, where I hope he is thriving.)

Or the time Benjamin transformed into a "fearsome pirate," complete with an eye patch and a cardboard sword. He led a full-scale preschool mutiny, culminating in a dramatic "walking of the plank" (off a chair, onto a pile of pillows).

Then there was the week the kids decided to open a restaurant in the dramatic play area. They took orders, made menus, and even created their own money. Emily, ever the perfectionist, memorized the entire menu and greeted her "customers" with impeccable manners.

One boy, however, kept trying to order pizza. The "chef," unimpressed, sighed and said, "Sir, we only serve soup here."

Moments like these reminded me why I had stumbled into this world in the first place. It was my dream to create a place where children were loved and happy, parents loved and trusted us, and teachers loved to work there.

But it wasn't all sunshine and perfectly portioned snack times.

There were licensing visits that felt more intense than corporate audits. I remember one particularly intimidating inspector arriving with a clipboard and an expression that could curdle milk. She measured everything, asked about safety protocols, and inspected our files with the diligence of a Supreme Court justice for hours!

Just as she was about to leave, she noticed a child's drawing taped to my office wall. It was a little out of place with the rest of the décor.

"What's this?" she asked.

"It's a dinosaur," I said. "One of my students drew it for me."

She studied it for a moment. Then—she smiled. "You know," she said, "I think you're going to do just fine."

And just like that, I knew I was on the right path.

But the cherry on top? Our little school shared a block with a senior assisted living facility. And let me tell you, there's just something utterly magical about the connection between the tiniest humans and the wisest ones. The residents would come over during our reading time, nestling into kid-sized chairs as honorary storybook readers. And as our little learners grew more confident, the roles flipped—our students started reading *to* their new "grandmas" and "grandpas." Cue the collective melting of hearts. One holiday season, one of our beloved "grandpas" hand-carved tiny wooden cars—one for *every single child.* Every. Single. One. That's when I realized: not all partnerships are about profit margins. Sometimes, the best business relationships are measured in shared stories, wooden toys, and memories that bridge generations.

I always say that starting a business can feel like you've been dropped into the middle of a maze with no map, no flashlight, and definitely no cheat codes. It's lonely sometimes—there's no welcome packet or magic crystal ball to tell you you're on the right track. And oh, those sneaky little "what-if" thoughts? They love to show up uninvited, usually around 2 a.m., and try to eat your confidence for breakfast. *What if I can't pay the loan back? What if this whole thing crashes and burns? What if I hire the wrong people and everything spirals?* But the biggest, heaviest one for me? *What if I let my family down?*

Every entrepreneur has wrestled with the what-ifs. But the real magic happens when you flip the script: instead of "what if it *doesn't* work?" you ask, "what if it *does*?" Deep down, in the place where gut feelings live and caffeine can't reach, I *knew* I had something special. So, I made it my mission to become a professional dream-surrounder—handpicking people who believed in what I was building. Some believed so hard, it lit up the room. Others… well, they faked it really well, and honestly, I'll take it.

At the end of the day, I had a secret weapon: those tiny humans. Putting their needs first was the fuel that pushed me miles beyond my comfort zone. So when the doubts came creeping in (and they always did), I'd close my eyes and picture a classroom full of laughter and light. That's when I'd ask myself a better question: *What if I succeed... and they get the magical start they deserve?*

Because early childhood education? It's not just a job. It's a front-row seat to magic. Kids are funny! They are hilarious! Full of wisdom and imagination. I mean, what other job fulfills your heart with so much life, smiles, and milestones on a daily basis?

Chapter 2: Building the Dream

T hen, just a few years later—almost accidentally—one school became two. Then three.

At our peak, we had around 200 children enrolled at a time at each center, and throughout 15 years, more than 10,000 full- and part-time little ones passed through our doors. I went from managing a couple of employees to managing a full-scale operation with over 150 team members at once, including teachers, directors, and administrators.

We became the heartbeat of the community—a place where parents felt safe leaving their children, where kids thrived, and where teachers actually wanted to work. (We even had a waitlist for teachers!)

So, one idea turned into... well, let's just say it multiplied faster than Play-Doh crumbs on a carpet. What started as a small, "what if" thought grew into something much bigger. Before I knew it, I went from "Miss Ashli" with a handful of kids to "Owner Ashli" with a waiting list longer than the line for a new Disney ride.

How did it happen? A mix of sheer determination, a dash of madness, and an unhealthy amount of coffee.

***

In all honesty, there wasn't just one quiet little *"aha!"* moment when it hit me that we needed a second location. Oh no. This wasn't some gentle realization where I sipped my coffee, gazed thoughtfully out the window, and thought, *"It's time."* For me, it was more like a series of increasingly loud, slightly chaotic alarms blaring, all screaming at once: *"You need more space, lady!"* Let me walk you through a few of the moments that made it impossible to ignore.

First up? The waitlist. Oh, that waitlist. What starts as a proud little victory, *"Look at us! We're in demand! Yay!"* can very quickly morph into something out of a nightmare. At first, it was simple: a couple of post-its on my desk. Then, a whiteboard. Next, we graduated to a binder with tabs and handwritten names (because, you know, we were *fancy*). And before I knew it, I was managing multiple Excel spreadsheets like I was training for a Microsoft certification. My office walls were plastered with sheets of paper (names, ages, desperate parent notes like *"Please, my child needs to be here!"* or *"I go back to work on the 15th"* or *"My parents fly home next week and I have no one to help."*) Our hearts ached for them. If only the second school would hurry up and build itself! The list didn't just feel long. It became a full-time job managing it. Parents would call weekly, sometimes daily, just to check their status. I started recognizing voices before they even introduced themselves. The tipping point came one Tuesday when I went to jot down a new inquiry and realized that every surface in my office was already covered. We weren't just full. We were bursting

15

at the seams. Either we build another school… or I was going to need a much, *much* bigger binder.

And then there was the parking lot. What I once thought of as a decent-sized lot transformed into a daily scene of vehicular gymnastics. Drop-off and pick-up became an Olympic event. It wasn't a parking lot anymore. It was a full-on ballet of near-misses, honks, and parents pulling off desperate three-point turns while waving goodbye to their kids. I watched parents circle like vultures looking for a spot, park on the curb blocks away, or just hover with their hazard lights blinking.

One morning, a parent abandoned their running car right in the driveway, dashed inside, and ran back out shouting, *"I'm just picking up!"* while five cars sat patiently trapped behind them. It was equal parts hilarious and horrifying, and a crystal-clear sign that our setup just wasn't cutting it anymore. We needed more space where parents could drop off their little ones without risking fender benders or a parking lot standoff.

With a waitlist long enough to wrap around the block (twice) and a steady stream of desperate parents calling daily, we had all the proof we needed. A second location wasn't just a good idea. It was survival. And honestly, we felt pretty confident it would be a hit from day one. We already had leads, calls, and a line of families basically saying, *"Just tell us where to send the deposit."*

So, it was time to put on our real estate hats and go location hunting. And this is where those casual business connections you've been nurturing suddenly become your secret weapon. We called up Mr. T, the same developer who'd helped us secure School #1's land, and laid out our wish list. We weren't picking blindly. We knew the area, had watched it grow, and saw firsthand that many of our current and future families were coming from there. New homes were sprouting up left and right. We needed to be right in the heart of that growth so that as families unpacked their moving boxes, they'd spot our school and think, *"Perfect!"*

Mr. T, being the gem that he is, rolled out his development maps and showed us a couple of promising spots, price tags included, of course. Then it was our turn. We took our notes, jumped in the car, and drove every potential site, channeling our inner preschool parent on the morning commute. We thought through everything. Traffic patterns, parking, coffee proximity (because let's be real, parents need that caffeine), the whole nine yards.

We crunched the numbers, drove up and down every nearby street, and finally made our pick: an undeveloped piece of land, right in our target zone. And the cherry on top? A future elementary school was planned just down the road. We were practically doing a happy dance in the car. To say we were excited would be a massive understatement. This was more than a win. It felt like the stars had aligned.

***

Walking into the second location project, my mindset was a whole different ballgame. I wasn't nearly as "alone" as I'd felt the first time around. This time, I had a

17

fantastic team backing me up, people I trusted, people who *got it*. My mantra through the whole process? *"We've got this!"* I was fluent in construction-speak (I could debate drywall types with the best of them), I knew every key player at the fire department, health department, and licensing office by name, and I probably could've recited the childcare rulebook backwards, in my sleep, without missing a beat. This time, I felt confident, knowledgeable, and ready to make decisions that actually made sense the first time.

And oh, did we put those hard-earned lessons to use. Every piece of feedback from School #1 went straight into the blueprint for School #2. Our teachers had (lovingly) grumbled about the lack of storage at the first location, because let's face it, tiny humans come with *a lot* of gear. So, we built an entire second floor dedicated to storage rooms and cozy lounge spaces. One teacher casually mentioned she wished we had a washer/dryer for those reading nook pillows she hauled home every weekend. Done. Washer/dryer room, installed. The kids had been dreaming of a bigger playground? You better believe we carved out tons of outdoor play space. We basically set out to build the smarter, souped-up version of School #1.

And while we're on the topic of building smarter, let me share a rookie mistake I see small businesses make all the time: waiting until the doors are open to start building buzz. Huge mistake. The minute we signed that land contract, up went the *"Coming Soon!"* sign, loud and proud, right on the fence. We called a team meeting to loop in our teachers first, because nothing beats having your own staff excited and spreading the word. Those teachers became our best cheerleaders, talking up the new school to future families and even potential hires.

Here's the thing. This isn't *Field of Dreams*. *"Build it and they will come"* is lovely in theory, but in reality? Not so much. A truly successful business starts marketing long before opening day. And if you can manage it like we did, start filling those waitlists a good three months before you plan to open. Future-you will want to give past-you a giant high five for making sure you hit the ground running.

***

When you're building a school, most people expect the budget battles to be over things like flooring, playground equipment, or maybe paint colors. Not me. No, my hill to die on was exotic granite for the foyer. My contractor, bless his practical, budget-conscious heart—just couldn't wrap his head around it. *"It's a school, ma'am,"* he'd mutter, probably picturing crayon smears and muddy sneakers all over that shiny surface. *"Why does the entry need to look so fancy?"*

Because, my friend, first impressions matter. Even if those first impressions come from toddlers who might try to lick the polished stone.

He clearly thought I was off my rocker, but I stood my ground. Finally, with a sigh that could've deflated a hot air balloon, he sent me to *his place* for these special slabs. That little adventure led me to what can only be described as the most unique granite shopping experience of my life.

Picture this: a sketchy part of town, after hours (because apparently the best granite hides during daylight). We pull into a dimly lit slab yard, with two sad little floodlights flickering like they were hanging on for dear life.

And there I was, armed with my phone flashlight, trying to inspect subtle veins and flecks of granite like I was on some secret mission. My contractor probably thought I'd officially cracked. But wouldn't you know it. We found *the* perfect slab. Who knew that spending thousands on stone, in near darkness, could be so thrilling? My sanity took a hit, but that foyer? It was going to be grand. Take note, contractors: never stand between a determined woman and her granite.

From signing to opening took about a year and a half. Sometimes it felt quicker than the first time, and other times it felt like a foggy déjà vu of endless permits, inspections, and walk-throughs. More than once, I found myself muttering, *"Ohhh rightttt, we have to do that again."* But in the end, every hurdle was worth it.

And because we were feeling fancy, we decided to flip the layout for School #2. We gave our older kids' classrooms access to the bigger playground. Seemed logical! But that one design change? It completely stumped our construction crew. Somehow, they managed to install teeny-tiny toddler toilets in the classrooms meant for our big kids. I'm talking about potties for tots still mastering walking— not for pre-K giants ready to take on the world.

When I (gently) pointed out the minor, but oh-so-critical plumbing fail, they had to rip out those adorable but totally wrong toilets and replace them with the proper size. And what did that leave us with? A pile of perfectly good, brand-new little potties we couldn't use. The project manager stared at me, bewildered, and asked, *"What would you like me to do with these? We can't return them."* My brilliant response? *"Stick 'em in storage!"* Because as any business owner knows, you never throw out a perfectly good (if hilariously misplaced) asset. You never know when it'll come in handy.

Sure enough, back at School #1, we were facing a classic preschool dilemma: a group of older kiddos who were ready to move up... except for one thing. They hadn't quite conquered potty training. And then it hit me—our potty party moment! We hauled one of those pint-sized thrones from storage, plunked it down as the star of our new *Potty Party,* and let the magic happen.

Oh, it was a hit! The kids were thrilled, taking turns on their very own special potty, showing off their potty skills like champions, and pretending to flush with gusto. Parents cheered louder than at a little league game, we danced the potty dance (yes, it's a thing), and we handed out shiny new underwear as prizes. And wouldn't you know it? Within a week or two, most of those formerly reluctant kiddos were totally ready to transition. Sometimes the universe gives you lemons, or in this case, the wrong toilets—and you turn them into pure potty-training gold. And that, my friends, is how our infamous Potty Party tradition was born!

***

So, how did the community react to the shiny new second school? Well, let's just say we had them buzzing like a hive of very excited bees before the doors were even open! We weren't exactly shy about our plans. We jumped into local moms' groups on social media, gave sneak peeks during tours at our first location, and painted a vivid picture of the awesome space we were building. And here's where we got really clever: some families enrolled at School #1 with the express plan to transfer to School #2 the minute it was ready. We had a built-in fan club before a single wall went up. The excitement was real, and honestly? We were feeling pretty confident that we'd fill that place faster than my son belts out the ABCs—skipping half the letters, of course.

And then—because no small business journey would be complete without a surprise twist—our competition decided to crash the party. Just a couple of months before our grand opening, another preschool opened *right* near our new location. Suddenly, it felt like someone had let the air out of our perfectly inflated balloon. They scooped up some of our leads and initial enrollments—especially from parents who needed care *right now* and couldn't wait for our doors to open. It stung. There we were, ready to roll, and boom—curveball.

But here's the classic small business lesson (usually learned the hard way): competition doesn't care about your timeline. You can have the best pre-marketing, the longest waitlist, the most loyal fans—but if another option opens sooner, and parents are in a pinch, they'll go where they have to. It forced us to take a breath, sharpen our message, and really own what made us different.

Spoiler alert? We got our kids back.

Because at the end of the day, what we built spoke for itself. We opened, found our rhythm, and watched as many of those families found their way back to us. Why? Because they realized what truly mattered. While others were busy cramming as many kids as possible into classrooms, we kept our ratios low. Our teachers weren't there to herd; they were there to nurture. We weren't just filling spots—we were building relationships. We knew our kids' quirks, their triumphs, their favorite colors, their least favorite vegetables. We built a community, not a crowd. And when it comes to your most precious little humans? That matters. Quality, care, and connection will always win over *just being open now.*

And speaking of connection, let me tell you about one of my favorite moments from that time.

About a week after we shared our big news with our team, we announced it to our families. There were lots of *"Congratulations!"*, a few nervous jokes about *"Don't you dare take my child's teacher over there!"*, and one dad who casually asked if his tuition was about to go up to pay for it. (Points for honesty.)

Now, preschool parents talk. Oh, do they talk. And sometimes your best marketing comes from the most unexpected places.

One day, in the middle of all the buzz, Mr. Frank—a dad at our school—poked his head into my office. *"Do you have a minute?"* Now, let me tell you, that question always made me nervous. You never knew if you were about to hear a compliment, a complaint, or get asked about the snack menu.

Mr. Frank was a man of few words, with a poker face so unreadable you'd think he was guarding state secrets when he was just asking about nap mats. We didn't even dare call him by his first name. It was always *"Mr."* Frank. So imagine my surprise when he walked in and... actually smiled.

"Hey, Mr. Frank!" I said, trying to sound cheerful and not at all like my heart was pounding, wondering what was coming.

He stepped inside and said, *"Heard from the Johnsons the other day."* His voice was as flat as the Texas plains.

My ears perked up. The Johnsons—we'd just toured them a few days prior. *"Oh really?"* I said, trying to sound casual but bracing for anything.

And in that same unreadable tone, he delivered the gold: *"They were asking where to send their kids. Told 'em,*

'Look, if you want 'em to learn somethin' and actually like going to school, you send 'em here. My kid doesn't complain, and that's sayin' somethin'.' You'll probably be hearing from 'em."

Then he nodded, said, *"Let me know,"* and walked out, leaving me standing there grinning like I'd just won the lottery. No fanfare, no flowery speech—just the highest compliment a man like Mr. Frank could give: *"My kid doesn't complain."*

It's a reminder I've carried with me ever since. You never know who's quietly singing your praises, or how one simple, genuine comment can lead to your next enrollment. Sometimes, the most powerful testimonials come from the quietest voices.

***

Going from one school to two was like trading in your cozy family minivan for a roaring full-sized tour bus. Or, in preschool-speak, going from one-on-one defense to zone coverage. It was exciting, chaotic, and full of new opportunities, along with the occasional head-scratching moment that had me wondering if I needed a referee whistle instead of a walkie-talkie.

One of the major wins with School #2 was that we actually had the luxury of hiring early. I mean, really early. We weren't scrambling last-minute, begging for warm bodies. We were strategically building a dream team while School #1 was still running full tilt and #2 was still very much in "hard hat" phase. The first star to join that crew? Ms. Rebel. She applied for an office position, downplayed her skills with that soft-spoken charm of hers, and within what felt like five minutes, we'd promoted her to co-director. She was sharp, positive, and an instant culture fit. One of those rare finds who doesn't just do the job but elevates everyone around her.

So, with Ms. Rebel at my side, we dove into interviews, and our new hires got the VIP training treatment. Immersed right into the established rhythm of School #1. They weren't just getting a feel for our curriculum; they were soaking in the essence of what made our school tick. Toddler tantrums? Observed and learned. Parent conferences? Shadowed and survived. The art of executing a theme day without losing your mind? Mastered. By the time School #2 was ready to open, these new hires weren't newbies. They were already steeped in our values and ready to hit the ground running.

Of course, every silver lining has its cloud. And ours came in the form of a very crowded School #1. We had new teachers and admin staff all mingling with our seasoned crew. And let's just say, it didn't always go off without a hitch. It was like putting too many chefs in a preschool kitchen... and then watching them debate the best way to sing the cleanup song.

One unforgettable morning, I walked in on a standoff between Ms. Rachel (OG from School #1) and Ms. Alma (rising star from School #2) over who got to lead circle time.

"Good morning, ladies!" I said, a little too cheerily.

Ms. Rachel, arms crossed, replied, "Just discussing our pedagogical approaches to 'Wheels on the Bus.'"

Ms. Alma, foot tapping: "Mine incorporates more gross motor skills."

Ms. Rachel: "Mine has historical accuracy."

I blinked. "Historical accuracy... for a bus song?"

Yep. We needed better structure and maybe a referee. We created formal training times, gave everyone breathing room, and learned the hard way that even passionate teachers need space (and maybe a shared Spotify playlist for group songs).

The admin staff had their own version of turf wars. Our humble little breakroom (read: supply closet with a mini fridge) became a battleground over filing systems. Alphabetical vs. classroom-based. Tempers flared. Folders were waved. I popped my head in and suggested a combo system, and you'd think I had asked them to calculate toddler tax returns.

Despite the drama, the growth was worth it. These new hires lived through our culture before stepping foot in their new home base. They carried that spirit with them, becoming instant culture-bearers at School #2.

Now, speaking of staff legends, let me tell you about one of my absolute favorite events: International Night. It's a school-wide celebration of different cultures where every classroom picks a country to highlight. The hallways explode with music, food, crafts, and joyful chaos.

That year, Mr. Forest, a thoughtful, steady teacher, chose Korea, knowing that one of his students, Aiden, had family roots there. Aiden was a shy little guy, hesitant to speak up even on the best days. But Mr. Forest had a quiet plan. He looped in Aiden's parents, and together, they turned the classroom into a miniature Korean cultural centre, complete with traditional hanboks, musical instruments, and ceramics.

At first, Aiden just pointed at things as his parents explained. But soon, whispers turned to soft words, and by the time International Night rolled around, Aiden was *explaining* things. He stood proud beside a table of artifacts, telling other families about the drum his grandfather used to play and the fan his mom brought from her childhood home. His confidence blossomed in front of our eyes. It wasn't just about learning a culture. It was about belonging, empowerment, and seeing a child shine. That, to me, is the heart of what we do.

Having teachers like Mr. Forest made everything that our school stood for come alive for both the children and the families (and made our directors' jobs a piece of cake, as teachers like him needed more encouragement rather than coaching and disciplining). Another such amazing teacher was Mrs. Yaseen. An absolute pleasure to work with, when she told us her two sisters were looking for jobs as well, we jumped on the opportunity! Now... let me confess a classic mistake. We got too excited. In our heads, we had already filled our open positions with mini-me's of Yaseen. We fast-tracked both of them through hiring. Lesson: just because one sibling is fantastic doesn't mean the rest are plug-and-play.

At first, the three were inseparable. But then Clara, the eldest, started challenging policies like she was auditioning for a reality show. One-hour lunch? Optional. Personal days? Claimed like candy. Feedback? Not her favorite concept. She eventually stormed out after a formal warning, leaving a dramatic hole in our staff chart. And wouldn't you know, within a week, the work ethic of the other two sisters took a nosedive. We had to reassign one and part ways with the other. Lesson learned: vet everyone. Thoroughly. And always keep your standards crystal clear.

While I was going through the process of choosing the dream team for my schools, I found myself on another learning tangent, leadership-wise, mainly. I realized there was much growth I had yet to embrace. I went from being everywhere, doing everything, to trusting others to carry the baton. Delegating? Oof. Not easy. I tried letting Annie plan our Parent Appreciation Night. A job I adored. Her theme? "All Things That Go." I silently cringed. But come event day, the place was *packed* with real trucks, fire engines, ambulances, and monster trucks. Parents were in awe. Annie looked at me, beaming: "Told you to let go. We've got your back."

And you know what? They did. I learned that when you give people room to lead, they surprise you in the best ways.

Communication, though, was a beast. A snack policy update got hilariously lost in translation between me, Annie, and Ms. Kate, leading to a juice debacle and some very confused teachers. That moment taught me: no more casual relays. Structured systems, clear emails, and regular leadership check-ins became non-negotiable.

The biggest takeaway? I didn't just need to lead, I needed to *build* leaders. And the only way to do that was to step back, trust, and create space for my team to step up, shine, and sometimes, just sometimes, rent a monster truck.

***

Now, let's talk about what no one really warns you about when you're expanding a business: the toll it takes on your family life. Sure, we're taught how to budget, build, market, and lead, but no one hands you a guidebook titled, "How to Not Miss Your Kids Growing Up While Chasing Your Dreams."

All the fast and furious expansion took its toll. On my marriage, on my kids, and on me. Yes, my boys thought the construction trucks and machinery were the coolest thing ever during the build-out of School #2. They'd press their little faces against the windows, utterly fascinated. But what they didn't love? How often Mommy wasn't home.

My husband found himself playing both mom and dad more than either of us had bargained for, and while he did it with love and strength, I could feel the strain. I tried—oh, I tried—to make it to every event, every game, every class party. But the reality was, there were days I had to send my parents or in-laws in my place because I had to be there for one school or the other.

The breaking point? It came a few months after School #2 opened. One day, I had to open one school before sunrise and close the other long after sunset. I didn't see my kids that entire day. Not one hug. Not one story. Not even a sleepy-eyed goodbye in the morning. I missed it all. And I was devastated. That night, I sat on the edge of my bed, still in my work clothes, heart aching, and I made myself a promise: this wasn't sustainable. Something had to change.

And change it did. Within a couple of months, I restructured our leadership model. Each school had its own robust management team—one had a Director and an Assistant, the other had two Co-Directors. And Annie, my trusted partner and total rockstar, got promoted to Executive Director, overseeing both locations. She was thrilled, and my team stepped into their roles with a level of ownership and pride that made my heart burst.

As for me? I took back my mornings. I became "Mom" again. I had breakfast with my boys. I drove them to school. I picked them up. I re-entered the rhythm of their daily lives—not as the woman who sometimes showed up, but as the constant they deserved. It only took a few months to course-correct, but those months made all the difference.

And yes, the boys were always involved in the schools from day one, especially Parker, my youngest. He was just 18 months old when we opened our first school, and boy, did that tiny tornado keep things interesting. Having him there shaped not only the vibe of our program but my entire approach as an owner.

Being both a mom and the school owner was the ultimate lens of accountability. Every hiring decision went through one simple filter: Would I want this person teaching Parker? If the answer wasn't a resounding, firework-filled, absolutely-yes, then it was a no. He was my quality control. My little tester. And if someone wasn't good enough for him, they weren't good enough for anyone else's child either. That's how deeply I believed in leading with care.

But Parker's presence also meant I had to develop a very special skill set during those early days: stealth. Because if Parker saw me during a school tour? Game over. Immediate waterworks. "Mommy! MOMMY!" echoing through the halls like a siren, setting off a domino effect of tears across classrooms. Suddenly, the school didn't look like a peaceful haven of early education. It looked like toddler mayhem.

So, I got creative. Mid-tour, I'd drop into full crouch mode, scuttling past Parker's classroom windows like a ninja avoiding detection. I could give a compelling explanation of our inquiry-based curriculum while simultaneously army-crawling beneath a toddler-sized easel. It wasn't exactly dignified, but hey, it worked.

Years later, I stood in front of Parker's graduating pre-K class, giving the speech, and I had to laugh. I actually apologized to the parents for all the incident reports they'd received. Not because of their kids, but because of Parker's latest mischievous escapade. That boy was into everything. But he was also my why. My purpose. And his presence reminded me, every single day, why we were doing what we were doing.

That's what I tell other preschool owners now: this work is personal. So incredibly personal. Parents are entrusting us with their most precious little humans, and with their hard-earned money. You better believe that if Blake's beloved cuddle toy goes missing, we're launching a full-scale search like it's the moon landing. The small stuff? It's the big stuff to them. And when you truly understand that, customer service becomes a no-brainer.

Because at the end of the day, these aren't just schools. They're communities. They're families. And if my own family taught me anything during those growing pains, it's that presence, not perfection, is what matters most.

***

Let's not sugarcoat it. There were days I seriously considered submitting my own resignation letter. The kicker? There was no one to submit it to. That's the hilarity and heartbreak of being your own boss. You're the CEO, the janitor, the HR department, and the one who has to talk yourself off the ledge at 3:00 AM when the ceiling is staring back at you, mocking your life choices.

Running two schools wasn't just double the responsibility. It was triple the pressure, quadruple the emotional load, and, if we're being honest, about twelve times the caffeine. There were so many moments during the early days of School #2 when the weight of it all nearly crushed me. The construction delays, budget overruns, staffing headaches, and that ever-present whisper of self-doubt. I'd catch myself wondering, "Was this a brilliant move or a well-dressed breakdown in progress?"

But what pulled me through? My tribe. My people. My family who believed in me even when I barely believed in myself. My friends who listened patiently as I vented about HVAC issues and enrollment numbers. And my team, the brilliant, resilient, hilarious team of kind-hearted educators who reminded me every day why we do what we do. The teacher who left a card on my desk calling me her superhero. The parent who thanked us for turning drop-off tears into joyful skips. The toddler who wrapped their arms around my leg and whispered, "You're the bestest, Miss Ashli." Those aren't just feel-good moments; they're fuel. When you're running on fumes, those moments light the fire again.

And then there were the big, beautiful, completely unexpected traditions that formed along the way. Like our anniversary celebrations. At School #1, it became this warm and fuzzy reunion complete with pony rides, throwback slideshows, and alumni who towered over me but still remembered our classroom chicken puppet. At School #2? It was a vibrant future-forward extravaganza. Think robots, space themes, and budding scientists in glittery lab coats.

Two schools. Two personalities. One mission: celebrate growth, community, and the magic of childhood.

What surprised me most in the jump from one school to two? That one plus one doesn't equal two. It equals a whole new dimension of leadership. With School #1, I was hands-on. Present. Queen bee of the hive. But add a second location, and suddenly I was everywhere and nowhere all at once. I couldn't physically be in both buildings, and the guilt was real. If I was at one, I felt like I was neglecting the other. My brain felt like a tab overload on a browser with zero RAM.

I had to delegate. Fully. Authentically. Relinquish control in a way that was terrifying but so necessary. My role shifted from hands-on manager to coach, visionary, and culture keeper. I inverted the management pyramid, putting my directors and teachers at the top, and myself as the support system underneath. They made the magic happen. I provided the stage, the script, and the spotlight.

And oh, the communication curveballs. What used to be a hallway chat now required emails, folders, and scheduled leadership meetings. We had one comically disastrous moment where one school ended up with enough pipe cleaners to construct a zoo, while the other school was rationing googly eyes like they were diamonds. Lesson learned: clarity and structure are everything when you can't be in the room.

Of course, there was doubt. So much doubt. Mostly from me. Could I really replicate that special School #1 culture? Was I being reckless or brave? But I leaned into intentionality. We trained new staff at School #1 before they ever stepped into #2. We cross-pollinated culture through team events. We celebrated old traditions and let new ones blossom organically. Like the infamous School #2 Dress-Up Days, where the teachers once arrived in coordinated avocado costumes just because it was Tuesday. I didn't try to force one school's identity onto the other. I let each one find its rhythm.

And the leadership lessons? Whew. I could write a book on just that. (Oh wait, here we are!) I learned to be the duck: calm on the surface, paddling like mad underneath. I learned to trust my people deeply and without micromanagement. I learned that customer service in childcare isn't about policy. It's about the missing cuddle toy, the forgotten show-and-tell item, the moment a child needs comfort and someone notices. That's the magic.

In the end, it wasn't the spreadsheets or the perfectly executed drop-off schedules that kept me going. It was the community we built. The culture we cultivated. The lives we touched, child by child, moment by moment. And when that inner skeptic gets loud, I look around and see a whole ecosystem we created together. Then I smile, hug my coffee mug a little tighter, and whisper to myself, "You did that. Now let's go do it again."

***

Despite all the chaos that came with expanding to a second location: the long days, the spreadsheets threatening to unionize, the emotional rollercoaster of toddler hugs and parking lot jousts, there was one thing that remained absolute, and that was our mission. Our core values stood like unshakable pillars, even as we doubled in size, team, and sometimes stress levels. We were still in the business of love, care, and education. Period.

No matter how many buildings we occupied, or how many hats I wore on a given Tuesday, every single decision, big or small, was filtered through the same sacred lens: "Is this in the best interest of the children?" That question became our guiding star, our magic compass. And honestly, it made the hard decisions a whole lot easier. When you strip away all the noise, logistics, and adulting, that pure north always pointed us in the right direction.

Whether it was hiring, classroom structure, snack policy (yes, even Goldfish vs. fruit cups), or handling parent concerns, we always came back to that central truth. And because of that, our community felt the difference. Parents didn't just enroll their children in a school; they joined a family. A slightly chaotic, always passionate, glitter-dusted family that knew every kid's quirks and every parent's coffee order.

Now, if I could time-travel back to pre-Location-Two me, the one high on possibility and maybe a bit low on sleep—I'd offer a few choice words. First off: breathe. Deeply. And then I'd say, "Hey, girl, enjoy the journey." Because that's the part no one really tells you: how fast it all moves. How something that once gave you ulcers becomes a funny story in hindsight. How what once felt like the edge of the world becomes a well-worn memory, softened with time.

I'd also whisper, "Delegate sooner." Truly. One of the best things I did, and one I should've done earlier, was learn to trust my team. Given the opportunity, a shared vision, and a sprinkle of support, people will step up in ways that will make your heart swell. Delegation isn't a sign of giving up control; it's a sign that your vision is strong enough to stand on many capable shoulders.

And above all, I'd remind myself: stay rooted in the why. The reason we opened School #1 wasn't to chase growth or status. It was to create a place where children thrived, where families felt seen, and where educators felt proud. That mission didn't evolve. If anything, it deepened. Because with each new classroom, each new child's name to learn, and each new parent's trust placed in us, the importance of sticking to that mission became more powerful than ever.

So yes, the spreadsheet tabs multiplied, and yes, I once held a staff meeting from the floor of my mom-sized SUV. But the heart? The heart of our work stayed steady. And honestly, that's the part that matters most.

***

Going from a one-woman show to managing a team was like learning an entirely new language, one filled with phrases like "professional development," "conflict resolution," and "who called in today?"

I'll never forget my first team meeting at the new location, where we toured our new construction site first. It was a mix of eager newbies, seasoned pros, and a couple of people who seemed genuinely surprised they had shown up. We talked about curriculum, safety procedures, and the importance of a good sense of humor. I *tried* to project confidence, but inside, I was just hoping no one realized I was making half of it up as I went. I was nervous about how I would ever be able to repay my loan.

I wanted to create a place where teachers felt *valued*. So, we did potlucks, craft nights, and even the occasional impromptu dance party. Because happy teachers make for happy kids, and happy kids make for happy parents. And happy parents... well, they tell their friends.

Here's another tip for all my preschool owners: Hire the personality! Yes, the resume with the credentials and experience is also important, but when it comes to kids, you want teachers who will naturally go above and beyond for what is in the best interest of their children.

Chapter 3: The Neighborhood Gem

Deciding on a third school location should've felt like routine by now. But of course, the universe had different plans. When my father and I sat in our developer's office staring at a future map, he pointed to a spot that was basically... well, dirt. Empty, churned-up, absolutely barren dirt. And somehow, we said yes.

Most people would've seen a dusty field. We saw promise. We lived in that master-planned community, so we had front row seats to its growth. We knew homes were going up so fast they were practically selling off blueprints. Families were arriving by the truckload. The demand was coming, loud, proud, and hungry for childcare. And nestled next to our site on the map? A future elementary school. If you know preschool placement, you know that's a goldmine. Built-in longevity. Built-in families. Built-in trust.

And the icing on the cake? This site sat in the same general area as our other two schools. These were our people. We knew the families, the commute patterns, the school pick-up chaos. We weren't betting on a market. We were building in our own backyard, for a community we already loved and understood.

Designing School #3 came with a swagger that only comes from experience, and a few construction scars. At this point, we weren't just winging it. We had ideas, data, and maybe a Pinterest board or two. One big shift? Location vibes. While School #1 was nestled in a bustling commercial zone, and School #2 sat on a main thoroughfare, School #3 was planted deep inside the heart of a residential neighborhood. That meant integration, not just access. It needed to feel like a warm, welcoming part of the neighborhood—not a random business plunked down among homes.

We also learned our lesson from School #2's two-building shuffle. For School #3, we were determined to keep everyone under one roof. Infants, preschoolers, after-school kids, one unified layout, one flowing space. It boosted cohesion, simplified communication, and meant fewer sprints across rainy parking lots with clipboards.

Now, don't worry. I didn't forget the granite. By this point, my love for a fancy foyer was legend. My contractor, Bill, didn't even argue. He just sighed, mumbled something about "fancy school people," and handed me the stone catalog. But the real crown jewel? We laid the groundwork for a future splash pad right in our construction phase. Plumbing, drainage, electrical, all baked into the initial build. We didn't install it right away, but it was there, quietly waiting to bring splashy joy on some future sunny day. That kind of foresight? It made me feel like a full-on preschool architect genius.

Speaking of genius, let's talk playgrounds. With space tight, we turned to a landscape architect to help us design a multi-level playground. We're talking a true child wonderland with little climbing zones, shaded nooks, and sensory-rich corners. It wasn't just a place to burn energy, it was built for exploration and adventure. Tucked into the neighborhood, it became this cozy backyard paradise that sparked imagination from the minute kids ran out the back doors.

But as always, where there's construction, there's chaos. Cue our unexpected antagonist: the back neighbor. This woman launched a full-scale protest against our fence, convinced our preschool would become some sort of ball-throwing, noise-blasting nightmare that would ruin her peace. She skipped the HOA meeting but still managed to spark enough drama that we had to scrap our landscaping budget and install a higher, heavier, less-than-charming concrete wall just to keep the neighborhood peace. Not exactly the whimsical touch we hoped for, but hey, sometimes diplomacy looks like a privacy barrier.

The foundation remained unshakably familiar: families who deeply valued quality, care, and a true educational partnership. These weren't just people looking for a safe place to drop off their kids; they were parents looking for a school that aligned with their hopes and dreams for their children. That shared value system made the transition seamless. Even after the hurricane delayed our opening, we had families, some of whom had already been part of our first two schools, waiting to transfer in as soon as we were ready. That vote of confidence? Priceless. It meant that from the first day, the laughter of little ones filled our classrooms as it had always been meant to happen.

But what really set School #3 apart, and filled me with enormous pride, was how we staffed it. This time, most of our lead teachers didn't come from outside, they came from within. These were educators who had already walked the halls of Schools #1 and #2, already lived our philosophy, already knew that our version of "above and beyond" meant *way* beyond. Promoting from within gave us leaders who didn't just understand our standards—they carried them in their bones. That shared history gave School #3 a leg up from day one. These teachers weren't just walking into new classrooms; they were carrying the torch, lighting up a whole new space with the culture we'd worked so hard to build.

And while the demographics of this new location mirrored our first two schools. Highly engaged, education-focused families, and the master-planned community setting opened up new possibilities. Unlike the commercial zone of School #1 or the high-traffic edge of School #2, School #3 was nestled *within* the neighborhood itself. That meant more walks to the park, more collaborations with the HOA, more opportunities to participate in neighborhood events. It felt like we were growing with the community, not just operating beside it.

And then, just before our grand opening, nature decided to write a plot twist. A hurricane. That hurricane didn't just delay our launch, it cracked our hearts wide open and reminded us what schools *really* are. Not just places for learning, but anchors in times of chaos.

While many homes and businesses flooded, our school, thanks to a stroke of design genius and maybe a little divine favor, stood tall and dry. And so, we opened our doors... not to students, but to our neighbors.

In those surreal days after the storm, we became a donation hub. Our brand-new classrooms filled with food, water, clothes, diapers, and even microwaves. Strangers became teammates in our temporary relief center. Families who hadn't even enrolled with us yet showed up with extra canned goods and elbow grease. Parents from our other schools dropped off truckloads of supplies. We had volunteers sorting baby clothes in one room, and others setting up a makeshift appliance bank in another.

We even opened up our Wi-Fi and power supply to the public. You'd see neighbors sitting quietly in the hallway, charging their phones, FaceTiming relatives, or checking weather updates, grateful for a few minutes of connection and calm. I remember one dad coming in barefoot, having lost nearly everything in the flood. He didn't need a tour or a brochure. He needed a socket. We gave him that and a cup of hot coffee. He came back weeks later and enrolled his daughter.

But what really got me was the book drive.

Word had spread that many local teachers had lost their classroom libraries in the floods. So, we rallied. We sent out emails, posted on social media, and within days, the donations rolled in. Picture this: brand-new books, gently used favorites, crates filled with picture books, phonics sets, chapter books, all waiting to be adopted by teachers who had nothing left. I watched one young teacher cry as she picked out "Brown Bear, Brown Bear" and "The Snowy Day" for her kindergarteners. It was a powerful reminder that learning starts with love, and sometimes, love is a donated storybook.

Out of this disaster emerged one of the most beautiful, humbling experiences of my career. School #3 hadn't even officially opened its doors to students, yet it had already made its mark. We became more than a preschool. We became a village hub. We became hope.

It also solidified something we always believed but hadn't yet experienced at this level: a school is a pillar of its community, not just in the good times, but especially in the hard ones. No amount of branding or open-house flyers could create the kind of loyalty and belonging that formed in those flood-soaked days. Our staff, our families, and even people who hadn't heard of us before that week became part of something special. And that bond? It's stronger than any foundation we've ever poured.

**

Originally, the plan was to open right alongside the local school district's fall semester. Neat, tidy, and perfectly on brand. But then came the hurricane, quite literally blowing those plans out the window. Still, in true preschool-owner fashion, we pivoted, adapted, and leaned into community connection like never before. Because if we couldn't open the doors right away, we'd at least open hearts and freezers.

That summer leading up to the launch, our incredible Directors for School #3, Ms. Tanya and Ms. Violet, transformed into mobile marketing superheroes. Imagine this: two powerhouse women pushing a branded ice cream cart to the most popular neighborhood park and nearby splash pad, both just a stone's throw from our soon-to-open school. Kids squealed with delight as they were handed free cones in the sweltering heat, and while they licked their vanilla or chocolate treats, their parents got the real scoop, from upcoming programs to our school philosophy. That cart was our secret weapon. And guess what? It worked. Families were enrolling before we even had furniture in the classrooms.

Once our Certificate of Occupancy came through and construction wrapped up, we kicked things into high gear. We shifted those sweet socials onto school grounds. It was the ultimate trust-me pitch. Picture a nearly empty building, no toys, no chairs, maybe a few pieces of painter's tape still stuck to the floor, but oh, we had vision. We'd walk parents through echoing hallways with nothing but imagination and polished foyer counters to help tell the story. "Here's where the toddler classroom will be, complete with sensory bins and a dramatic play corner," I'd say, arms wide, as if summoning the furniture from thin air. Ice cream still in hand, parents would nod, and slowly, you could see it, the dream taking shape in their minds too.

Then came opening day, and with it, the weight of everything we'd overcome. We didn't tiptoe into our third school's story, we leapt in with a Fall Festival-themed grand opening bash that was nothing short of magical. We invited families and staff from all three schools to celebrate not just the new building, but the spirit of our community after an incredibly difficult storm season. It was loud, it was messy, it was colorful chaos of the best kind.

Our theme? Superheroes, of course. Because every teacher, parent, and child who weathered that hurricane, and the wild journey to get this school open, *was* a superhero. There were tiny capes, glitter face paint, a bounce house or two (okay, three), and nonstop laughter echoing through the playground. It wasn't just a school opening; it was a triumph.

And the ribbon-cutting? We don't do boring. We stretched a giant pink ribbon across the front columns of the school, and in one glorious, celebratory moment, every teacher lined up with scissors and cut it *together*. It wasn't about one person. It was about all of us. The entire team that had believed in the vision pushed through the delays and stood proudly ready to welcome the next chapter.

As for me? I didn't even hold the scissors. I handed them to my dad.

Because through every floorplan sketch, every concrete pour, every budget conversation (and debate about granite countertops!), he was right there beside me. This school was our shared dream. Watching him make that cut, surrounded by a sea of joyful families and our ever-growing team, was one of the most emotional and fulfilling moments of my career.

***

My relationship with my father during the third school project absolutely evolved. Working through one school together had been an adventure. Two made us co-conspirators. But three? That cemented us as partners in a way that only construction dust, financing meetings, and a shared love of control can do.

The truth is, building a school from the ground up with your dad is not your average family bonding activity. Most people grab coffee or go golfing. We reviewed architectural renderings and debated drainage slopes. We had started our commercial real estate company when we purchased the land and building for School #2, and by the time we reached School #3, that little venture had taken on a life of its own. It's still thriving today, branching into projects across a couple of states, which, yes, means even more opportunities for father-daughter "discussions."

At the core of our dynamic? Unshakable trust. He trusted me to make big, bold, sometimes budget-bending decisions in service of creating the most welcoming, thoughtful school environments. And I trusted him to raise an eyebrow when I needed grounding, to double-check every line item, and to always have my back, even when I was ordering light fixtures that cost more than he thought they should.

We had our moments. I can still hear him now, staring in disbelief at a sample of some stunning imported tile I'd fallen in love with. He held it up like it might bite him. "Do you know how many square feet of standard tile this could buy, honey?" he asked, somewhere between baffled and resigned.

I smiled. "But Dad… just *look* at it."

That was us in a nutshell, me pushing the aesthetic envelope, him clutching the budget with both hands. But underneath every debate about granite foyer counters and high-end cabinetry was a deep respect for what the other brought to the table. I wasn't just making things pretty for the sake of pretty, I was building an experience, a brand, a place where families would walk in and immediately feel safe, seen, and supported. And he wasn't just watching the pennies, he was ensuring our vision was sustainable, that we could keep building these havens for years to come.

We challenged each other, absolutely. But we never doubted each other. That push-and-pull became our rhythm, our language. He'd rein me in when necessary, and I'd stretch his comfort zone when I knew it mattered. And over time, those "discussions" turned into some of our best memories. Because when you're building something meaningful with someone who truly believes in you, even when you're being extra about the ceiling tile, there's a kind of magic in that.

Honestly, I think some of our strongest work didn't come from when we agreed immediately. It came from when we each brought our full selves, our convictions, our passions, and worked it out. Brick by brick. Meeting by meeting. Laugh by occasional exasperated sigh. And yes, I'll always fight for beautiful granite. But more than anything,

I'll always be grateful I got to build these dreams alongside my dad.

***

If there's a club for business owners, that's probably the most elite, and the most exhausted, membership, it's the burnout club. And decision fatigue? That's its clingy, ever-present sidekick. During the whirlwind of running School #1, hiring for #2, and overseeing the construction of School #3, I was basically functioning on caffeine, willpower, and a prayer. There wasn't a single hat I wasn't wearing. One minute I was in a staff interview, the next, approving fencing heights, then dashing into a toddler room to help with snack time. It was like juggling flaming torches on a unicycle while answering emails.

The worst part? The constant *deciding*. Every day was an avalanche of choices. Some big (budgets, staffing, safety regulations). Some absurdly tiny (red cups or blue for snack time?). And all of them landed squarely on my shoulders.

The final straw came on a Friday night. I came home, worn thin like a fraying shoelace, barely managing to collapse on the couch. My sweet, well-meaning husband took one look at me and said, "Love, you've had a long week. Let's go out. Where would you like to eat?"

And that... was the moment I snapped.

"Really?!" I barked, with the volume of a teacher who's just seen a toddler color on the wall in permanent marker. "Another decision?! That's one more question I have to answer! All day, it's been, 'Ms. Ashli, do you have a second?' 'Should we hire this teacher?' 'Does this water heater meet code?' 'Is the playground fence tall enough?' I swear, if one more person asks me anything, I'm going to scream."

Poor guy. He stood there like a deer in headlights, regretting his dinner offer more than any man in history. I think I even shouted something about wanting *someone else* to tell *me* what to do for once.

But then came the release. That strange kind of post-rant clarity. I took a breath, okay, several, and finally said, "Fine. Mexican. Mexican would be great."

And you know what? It *was* great. Margaritas were had. Laughter followed. And that moment, ridiculous as it felt, was my burnout breakthrough. A full-on, salsa-drenched meltdown that taught me a few things I now swear by.

First, flawless (or nearly flawless) organization became my mission. We created SOPs for everything. Communication templates. Workflow systems. The goal was simple: if it could be answered by a document, it shouldn't land on my desk. The more I empowered my team to find answers themselves, the lighter my mental load became.

Second, I leaned into the glorious art of delegation. True delegation, not the "you do it but check with me first" kind. I learned to let go, to trust that if I'd trained my team right, they didn't need me in every decision. It wasn't always easy, especially when I was used to being the human hub, but it was necessary. My job evolved from "do everything" to "guide the people doing everything." And guess what? They often did it better than I would have.

And third, accountability. I held my team to it, and myself. If I was handing off responsibility, I had to trust they'd carry it, and give them space to shine (or learn). That trust gave us all room to breathe.

Still, even the most color-coded Google Drive and best-laid org charts can't fix a soul on empty. So what really brought me back to purpose? Those quiet, shining reminders of *why* we do this. A child's proud drawing. A teacher's thank-you note. A parent's tearful, "you changed our lives." These weren't just sweet moments, they were lifelines. Proof that the hard stuff was building something worth every second of chaos.

And yes, making space for myself, reading, walking, even zoning out to bad reality TV, became non-negotiable. Because when you're the engine driving the whole train, running out of fuel isn't just inconvenient, it's dangerous. You have to protect your peace like it's the most important appointment on your calendar. Because some days, it absolutely is.

***

And speaking of the unsung heroes who keep the engine running, let me tell you about Oscar. Our handyman. Our behind-the-scenes MVP. If burnout taught me the value of delegation and support, then Oscar was the living, toolbelt-wearing embodiment of it. He wasn't just maintenance. He was a walking fix-it legend with a key ring so big it could double as a kettlebell. And somehow, no matter how chaotic things got or how many metaphorical fires I was trying to put out, Oscar was always there, calm, steady, and ready to climb a roof or flip a burger, depending on the day.

First off, let's talk about his keychain. The man carried keys like they were going out of style. I swear it had its own gravitational pull. Every door, every utility box, every random storage shed across every school. Oscar had the key. He even had keys for things I didn't know *had* keys. I used to joke that if a secret passageway ever revealed itself behind the toddler cubbies, Oscar would probably already have a key to it.

Our staff had what I'd lovingly call a "classic love-hate relationship" with him. We all adored Oscar because, quite frankly, he could fix anything. AC on the fritz? Oscar. Leaky sink? Oscar. Squeaky classroom door? Oscar. Playground gate not latching? Oscar. He was our go-to, our wizard behind the curtain, working his magic in quiet, miraculous ways.

But then... there was *Oscar Time*. See, Oscar moved to the beat of his own drum. You'd call with a Level 10 emergency, say, a busted air conditioning unit in July during a record heatwave, and Oscar would say calmly, "I'll get to it later." Which, in Oscar Time, could mean later today... or possibly next Tuesday. Unless, of course, the request came from my dad.

Oscar had a deep, unspoken loyalty to my father. My dad could whisper a request, and like a summoned genie, Oscar would show up within 20 minutes flat. It was honestly impressive. The rest of us? We'd wait. But my dad? Immediate service. I eventually learned to preface my requests with, "Hey Oscar, *Dad* said..." just to shave off a few hours.

Even with his mysterious timeline, Oscar always came through. He'd often show up late in the evenings after the schools had emptied out, quietly repairing, maintaining, tidying. You'd come in the next morning and realize the thing you'd given up hope on was suddenly good as new. He worked like a ghost, with a toolbox.

One of my absolute favorite Oscar memories came during one of our chaotic, joy-filled Fall Festivals. I was walking around, making sure nothing was on fire (figuratively and literally), when I noticed a familiar figure behind the grill. There was Oscar, stone-faced as always, flipping burgers and hot dogs for dozens of hungry parents. "Oscar! What are you doing?" I asked, genuinely surprised. Without missing a beat, he shrugged, still flipping burgers with precision. "Someone's gotta feed 'em, right?"

That was Oscar in a nutshell. Quiet. Capable. Unfazed. A man of few words, endless keys, mysterious timelines, and, apparently, pretty impressive barbecue skills.

He's still with us. Still the guardian of every doorknob and drain pipe. And no matter how many buildings we add or how fancy our schools get, there will never be another Oscar. He's the kind of teammate you don't just appreciate—you count on. Every single day.

***

Following the steady, behind-the-scenes presence of Oscar, the man with the magic keys and an unexpectedly great burger flip, you start to realize that the true fabric of a school isn't just made of lesson plans, granite foyers, or playground mulch. It's sewn together by people. People who quietly, consistently, show up. People who believe in what you're building, and make the intangible parts, the heart, the history, the meaning, come alive.

That truth hits the hardest on graduation day.

Pre-K graduation at our schools is always a bittersweet affair. There's pride, yes, tons of it, but also a twinge of loss. We've watched these little ones grow from waddling toddlers into confident kindergarteners, and suddenly, it's time to let them go. So to honor that enormous milestone, we decided to create a gift that was more than just a photo op or a token trinket. We gave them a time capsule. A living, breathing archive of their early years.

What began as a sweet idea turned into one of the most emotional traditions we ever implemented. Our incredible teachers, secret sentimental masterminds, began collecting every drawing, every scribble, every early science project from the moment a child entered our program. It wasn't just a folder with a few cute crafts. It was an entire binder, lovingly curated, tracing years of growth, imagination, and tiny triumphs.

One of the moments I'll never forget came during Olivia's graduation. Her parents were already glowing with pride, holding back happy tears as they watched her walk across the stage. But when we handed them that thick binder filled with Olivia's artwork, the emotions spilled over. Her mom flipped open to a crayon rainbow from the toddler room and just lost it. Tears of joy, awe, and something deeper.

After the ceremony, she pulled me aside, clutching the binder like it was made of gold. Through her tears, she said something I'll carry with me forever: "Olivia is our miracle baby. Two IVF rounds. Years of hoping, praying, waiting. And now… here she is. This—" she gestured to the overflowing binder, "—this is everything. Every page is a piece of her journey. Of our journey."

That was the moment it clicked, again. What we do isn't just education. It's memory-making. It's scaffolding childhood for parents who've longed for it, sometimes for years. That binder wasn't just art. It was legacy.

And those emotional ties? They don't fade with graduation. If anything, they deepen.

Over the years, we were blessed beyond measure to have teachers and families who didn't just pass through, they stayed. They grew with us. Moved with us. Believed in us, not just once, but three times over. That kind of loyalty? It's humbling.

The Becketts were one such family. They were there from the very beginning. Their eldest started with us back at School #1 when I was still juggling my toddler, Parker, and doing ninja crawls to avoid being spotted during tours. They loved it. So naturally, when their second was ready for preschool, and School #2 opened its doors, they joined us again, without hesitation, full of warmth and trust.

And then, the moment that truly made my heart swell: when their third child was old enough, and School #3 had just opened. Fresh paint still drying, furniture barely in place. They were there, binder-ready and beaming. No questions. Just faith. Faith in what we'd built, in who we were, and in what we'd continue to be for their family.

Their journey mirrored ours. First child with our first school. Second with our second. Third with our third. Each step forward, on their path and ours, taken together. That kind of parallel growth is rare. And beautiful. And deeply affirming.

Families like the Becketts remind us that this work isn't about expansion for expansion's sake. It's about relationships. It's about trust earned, not once, but again and again. And it's about knowing, without a doubt, that the community you're serving believes in the heart of what you do. Even when the walls are still going up and the playground grass isn't yet spread.

***

By the time School #3 was up and running, my role had changed a lot. I wasn't the one doing everything anymore. I was the one helping others do their best. I had moved from being hands-on all the time to being more of a guide and support for my team. And with more than a hundred people now on payroll, I had to learn fast what real leadership looked like across multiple schools.

One of the biggest lessons I learned was how important it was to get more efficient. We stopped doing things three different times at three different places. For example, new teacher orientations. What used to be a separate, time-consuming process at each school, turned into one joint training that saved time and helped everyone feel like they were part of one big team from the start.

And the growth started to pay off in other ways, too. We finally had enough size to get better deals and open more doors:

- **Vendor Discounts:** We were now buying enough supplies to qualify for big savings. Everything from crayons to cleaning products came at better prices because we were ordering in bulk.

- **Enrollment Flexibility:** If a parent called and one school was full, we could offer a spot at another school without missing a beat. That made families happy and helped us stay full.
- **Better Training:** We could now afford to bring in national-level speakers and training for our teachers. Before, that felt impossible. Now it was part of our regular schedule—and our teachers loved it.
- **Career Growth:** With three schools, our teachers had places to grow into. We had room for promotions, chances to work with new age groups, and opportunities to lead. It helped us keep great people and gave them reasons to stay.
- **Team Benefits:** With a bigger team, we qualified for better group rates on things like health insurance, dental, and retirement plans. That meant we could offer real support—not just a paycheck.

Our schools started to run smoother, our systems were stronger, and I finally felt like we had built something solid. But through all the new systems, trainings, and checklists, the heart of our mission never changed. The children came first. The teachers mattered. The families trusted us. And every choice we made, every little or big improvement, had to serve those core values.

Still, as we grew, I won't lie, there was always a little voice in the back of my mind asking: *Are we getting too big? Too "corporate?"* It's a fear that never fully went away. I never wanted our schools to feel like just another chain. I didn't want to lose the special little moments, the deep connections, the feeling that every child was known and loved.

So, I worked hard to protect the heart of our schools, even as we added more people and processes. That meant being extra careful about who we hired, especially for leadership roles. I wasn't just looking for experience. I was looking for heart. I wanted people who truly believed in what we were doing, who would love these kids like their own, and who would support their teams with the same warmth and care we built this on.

We also made sure each school had room to be its own version of our bigger dream. I didn't want them to feel like copy-and-paste buildings. I gave our Directors the freedom to make choices that worked best for their community while still sticking to our shared values. I stayed close to all of them, checked in often, and kept our goals clear, but I didn't micromanage. I trusted them to carry the torch.

And most importantly, we never stopped celebrating the "why." We kept sharing stories, the hugs, the thank-you notes, the wins, the sweet and silly things the kids said. We cheered each other on. We made time for laughter, team traditions, and meaningful moments. I still showed up to classrooms. I still knew the names of kids and their favorite toys. I still got my hands dirty when needed (and flipped my share of burgers at Fall Festivals, alongside Oscar).

Because no matter how big we got, we weren't just running schools. We were building relationships. We were showing up for families in real ways. And that, more than any system or spreadsheet, is what kept us grounded, and growing, the right way.

***

By the time we opened School #3, I thought I had a pretty good handle on what "success" looked like. Happy kids, strong enrollment, dedicated teachers, and a well-run operation. But then came a moment that reminded me why all the systems, vendor discounts, and leadership lessons really mattered.

One afternoon, as I walked through that beautiful granite-adorned foyer, Ethan's grandma stopped me. Ethan was one of our bright, curious little ones. A dinosaur-loving chatterbox who could talk your ear off about the difference between a T-Rex and a Velociraptor. His grandma, a kind woman new to the country, had tears in her eyes.

"Thank you," she said softly. I smiled, thinking she meant for the school itself, but then she explained. She and her husband had moved here from overseas to help their son raise Ethan. They didn't have a car. They didn't drive at all.

She glanced toward the front doors. "Because your school is so close to our son's house, we can walk. It's just a short walk with the stroller. If you were not here... Ethan, he would not be able to go to school. He would be home, all day."

It stopped me in my tracks. We'd chosen that location for practical reasons, close to a future elementary school, inside a master-planned community, but here was an entirely different impact. Without us being right there, Ethan wouldn't be with his friends, learning and exploring. He'd be at home, missing out on everything that was shaping him into the curious, social little boy we knew.

In that moment, all the budgeting headaches, construction delays, and sleepless nights felt worth it.

***

If I had to sum up School #3 in one phrase, it would be the "Neighborhood Gem." It was still built on the same heart and high standards as the first two, but it felt different. More like an extension of home. Being tucked right into the community gave it a closeness to the other locations, just by their geography.

And oh, did the parents claim it as their own. I'd seen parents get attached before. School #1 families loved its cozy feel, School #2 parents bragged about its space and layout, but with School #3, the loyalty was something else entirely. They didn't just love it, they defended it like it was a member of their family.

One day, I was scrolling through a local moms' Facebook group when I saw a post asking for preschool recommendations. The comments poured in, and then one mom mentioned that our school was "hard to get to" because of temporary construction detours. That's when the magic happened. Parents jumped in like they were storming a castle to protect their own.

"Hard to get to? It's a five-minute walk for half the neighborhood!" one wrote.

"Totally worth a tiny detour for teachers like that!" said another.

"My kid has thrived there—best decision we ever made."

I didn't have to say a word. They spoke for us, from the heart. That's when I realized. School #3 wasn't just ours anymore. It belonged to the community.

Each school had taught me something. School #1 taught me how to start from scratch, with passion as my only fuel. School #2 taught me how to scale and let go of some control. But School #3? That one drove home the lesson that when you're not just in a community but truly part of it, the connection runs deeper than any marketing or program could ever create.

It also reminded me that the little things we plan, like location, can make life-changing differences, even in ways we never expect. Families like Ethan's could walk to us. Parents wore our school pride like a badge of honor. And in the middle of it all, I learned the most important leadership lesson yet: trust your people, trust your process, and trust that the heart you've built into your work will keep beating, even when you're not in the room.

Standing there on the front steps one afternoon, watching parents chatting at pickup, toddlers proudly showing off their art projects, and Ethan racing past with his dinosaur under his arm, I realized this was exactly what we had been building all along. Not just schools, but places where families felt seen, supported, and truly at home. School #3 wasn't the end of a journey; it was proof that when you lead with heart, trust your team, and stay rooted in your purpose, the work takes on a life of its own. And as I locked up that evening, the laughter of the day still echoing in the halls, I knew deep down that this was only the beginning of something even bigger.

Chapter 4: A Day In The Life (Multiplied By Three)

U nlocking a school in the morning is like stepping into a world that hasn't quite woken up yet. It's quiet, almost sacred, a pause before the whirlwind begins. To me, it always felt like the calm before the storm, except this storm was full of giggles, snack crumbs, and the occasional glitter explosion. Walking into a dark, still building, flipping on the first light, it's almost eerie, like watching a favorite band rehearse without an audience. You know what's missing: the children, the heartbeat of the whole place.

The very first thing that hits you is the smell. Freshly mopped floors, the faint waxy scent of crayons, and this subtle sweetness that only a perfectly still preschool can carry. The sight? A clean slate. Chairs stacked neatly on tables, toys in their places, a hallway bathed in the soft glow of the sunrise. And for every teacher reading this, yes, it's also the perfect time to find that Hello Kitty lunchbox Susie Q has been missing for a week.

Our ritual was always the same. Step one: power on the Keurig. That first cup of coffee was non-negotiable. Step two: crank up the hallway music and dance-walk your way down the halls, flicking on lights and filling every corner with warmth. For me, this was when I whispered a little gratitude. Thankful that I got to do this work, for these little people, with this amazing team. Before the kids arrived, it was our chance to get every detail just right.

But let me tell you, these checklists weren't just about neatness. They were about safety. One morning, a teacher doing the playground walk-through spotted a snake coiled inside the treehouse. Thankfully, it was harmless. But what if a child had discovered it instead? That morning routine suddenly became more than habit. It was a lifeline.

The "openers," as we called them, were a special crew. They set the tone for everyone else. At one school, Mrs. Chrissy made it her mission to hide inspirational quotes around the building. Teachers would open a closet and find a note that read, *"It takes a big heart to shape little minds,"* or *"Be the change that you wish to see in the world."* At another school, Ms. Margaret would show up with breakfast tacos or decorate a classroom door for a birthday. Those little gestures weren't in any handbook, but they mattered. They filled the building with love before the first family even walked through the door.

And of course, the teachers had their own rhythm before the kids arrived. There were hugs, high-fives, sleepy "good mornings," and sometimes full-on pep talks. Nothing formal, just a quick, "We've got this," or an encouraging smile. The energy depended on who you caught in the hallway. Some were bright-eyed and ready to roll. Others, like poor Ms. Anya, who usually closed the night before, looked like they had lost a wrestling match with their alarm clock.

One morning stands out. Ms. Margaret, our resident ray of sunshine, bounced into the hall blasting a high-energy pop song from her phone. She danced from room to room, narrating her tasks like a Broadway star. Meanwhile, Ms. Anya, clutching her coffee like it was her last lifeline, squinted at her and muttered, "Margaret, it's not even 6 a.m. My eyelids are still in negotiations. Please, ten more minutes of silence." Margaret, of course, ignored her and switched the music to an even louder Latin beat with a shimmy thrown in. Anya finally raised her head, gave a glare sharp enough to stop traffic, and croaked, "I need a minute." They both cracked up, and Margaret offered to grab her first round of caffeine. It was their rhythm, one bursting with energy, one just waking up, but together, they made it work. That was the beauty of our team.

As for me, my mornings changed over the years in the most meaningful way. In the beginning, I was the one unlocking doors, disarming alarms, and turning on lights. Every checklist was mine. But as the schools grew and my Directors took on more, I gave myself the gift of stepping back. Suddenly, I wasn't just an owner. I was a mom again.

Instead of rushing to the school at dawn, I was making breakfast for my own kids, helping them find shoes, offering pep talks before a quiz, and soaking up those moments I'd missed in the early years. Dropping them off at their school became one of my favorite daily rituals. It was the shift from owner/mom to mom/owner, and it was everything I'd been working toward.

After my mom duties, I'd head into one of our campuses, coffee in hand, not just for me, but for my team. I memorized their orders and made sure they had their favorite drink waiting. It was a small thing, but in the preschool world, where two hours can mean a teacher calling out, a health inspector walking in, or a parent wanting a last-minute chat, that coffee meant, "I see you. I appreciate you."

Because the truth is, running a preschool isn't just about the kids. It's about the adults who show up for them every single day. And starting the morning with gratitude, caffeine, and maybe even a little hallway dance party was how we reminded ourselves: no matter what the day brought, we were in it together.

***

Oh, the drop-offs. It's the Pinnacle Event for People Watching! If mornings inside the school were about quiet routines and checklists, then drop-off was the main event. It was where all the planning, the safety checks, the hallway coffee, and the little pep talks collided with the real world of parents and children. Drop-off was unpredictable. You never knew if it was going to be quick hugs and smiles, or a full-on Broadway performance at the classroom door. And truthfully, that unpredictability made it one of the most memorable parts of each day.

Parents at drop-off are a wild card. Sometimes you get frantic apologies, sometimes a confession that leaves you laughing, and other times words so heartfelt they stay with you forever. One morning, a mom rushed in, frazzled and flushed, and practically deposited her little boy, Leo, into my arms along with his backpack. "He's all yours," she said, breathless. "I've done my part. He's had breakfast, he's wearing pants, and he's not actively on fire." Then she grinned, adding, "The pants part was a real nail-biter this morning. You're welcome." We both laughed, and just like that, the stress of her morning melted into honesty and humor. It was a reminder that every family has their own kind of chaos before they get to us.

Another time, a dad walked in with his daughter Chloe, who was wearing a glittery tiara, a superhero cape, and pajama pants under her dress. He leaned toward me, whispering with a tired smile, "I just want you to know, I tried. I failed at doing her hair, and the pajama pants were non-negotiable. My coffee hadn't even kicked in yet." I reassured him we'd help out with her hair, and he left looking relieved. That one moment captured the truth about parenting. It's about picking your battles and loving your kids exactly as they are.

And then there were the moments that pierced straight through to the heart. A mom of one of our newer students, Lily, came to me with tears in her eyes. Lily had struggled with separation anxiety, but that morning she'd woken up saying, "Mommy, I'm so excited to go to school and see my friends." Her mom looked at me and said, "That's the first time she's ever said that. I feel like you've given me my happy little girl back." In that instant, every budget fight, every sleepless night, every challenge was worth it. Because this wasn't just about running a school. It was about changing lives in small but powerful ways.

Of course, some parents turned goodbyes into full productions that became legendary among our staff. There was one mom whose farewell routine was so drawn out it became a ten-minute spectacle every single morning. It started sweetly enough—with kisses on both cheeks, a big hug, and a high-five. But that was just Act One. She'd step back for an air-high-five, then give a dramatic wave from the doorway, as if she were boarding a ship bound for another continent. Just when you thought it was finally over, she'd march to the viewing window, press her hand against the glass, and her child would come running for that final, touching hand-to-hand moment. By then, the teachers were exchanging looks and stifling laughs. We even started joking about taking bets on how many steps it would take before she finally made it to her car.

Then, on the opposite end of the spectrum, you had the lightning-fast parents. They had perfected the art of the stealth exit: slip in, hand off the child, vanish. Done. If I ever needed a getaway driver, I knew exactly which parents I'd call.

Not everyone was so subtle, though. One dad routinely hid behind cars in the parking lot just to peek in and make sure his son was okay. Another family's routine involved a full goodbye song, sung in English and Spanish, with a little dance for flair. The kids loved it so much that half the class would join in, making drop-off a group performance. And then there was the mom who could never quite leave. She'd drop her child off, come back with the forgotten backpack, then again with water bottles, then again for jackets. By the time she called the front desk to remind us about the weather, we were all smiling knowingly.

Some parents were natural-born dramatists. Their goodbyes looked like a scene from a movie. Sighs, tears, and long, longing looks as if their child was heading off to war instead of snack time. And then there were the ones who weren't ready to let go, even when their child clearly was. One mom, convinced her son Camden wasn't adjusting, would linger with worry in her voice. Meanwhile, Camden was happily playing, perfectly content. The truth was, it wasn't Camden struggling with separation, it was her.

And then, of course, came the pajama-clad "work from home" parents. Post-COVID, their numbers tripled. They'd stroll in with coffee in hand, kids in tow, sometimes in slippers, hand them off with a quick "Return policy's not valid till 3 p.m.," and disappear. Off to the gym, a Zoom meeting, or maybe back to bed. Honestly, no judgement. Their kids were safe, happy, and loved, and that's what mattered.

But one parent took the cake. His name was Mark, and he was what we lovingly called a "linger-er." His son Oliver would run into class without hesitation, but Mark wasn't ready to leave. He'd ask the teacher about snacks, curriculum, even crayons. He'd sit in the tiny chairs during free play just to watch. Finally, one of our teachers, Ms. Anya, saved the day by announcing circle time. Mark sighed, stood up, and said, "Well, that's my cue." Before leaving, he offered to volunteer at lunch, *every day*. We laughed and half-jokingly handed him an application. His heart was in the right place, and his love for the school was clear.

The truth is, there is no perfect drop-off. Every family has their patterns, their battles, their sweet goodbyes. Some are quick, some are dramatic, some are chaotic, but all of them come from the same place: love. And as Early Childhood Professionals, our role wasn't to judge, but to understand, to support, and to cherish those moments.

On a personal level, I saw myself in every parent. I knew their frantic mornings, their bittersweet goodbyes, their fierce desire to do what was best for their child. But as the years passed and my oldest son left for college, something shifted in me. I found myself holding onto the hugs from our preschoolers just a little longer. When I listened to parents laugh about pajama pants or cry through goodbyes, I understood them not just as an educator, but as a mom who would have given anything to have those mornings back. Time is fleeting, and those drop-offs, as chaotic or messy as they may be, are moments worth treasuring.

Of course, not every morning was heartwarming. Some mornings were pure chaos, what we lovingly called "Meltdown Mondays." Usually, after a long weekend, it was as if every toddler in the building agreed to lose it at the exact same time. One morning, two of our openers called out, and we had to pull in Ms. Lena, a floater who was used to working with older kids. We placed her in the Toddler classroom. A room she wasn't used to being in. She did her best, but within minutes a battle over a red crayon had erupted into full-scale chaos. One child was shrieking, another was coloring on sleeves, another was laughing hysterically, and block towers were toppling.

The Directors walked in to find three teachers wrangling toddlers, paperwork piled high, and a new family being onboarded in the middle of it all. It was madness. By nap time, the teachers collapsed in their chairs, sighed, and then started laughing. Because that's the thing, yes, it was exhausting, but you always came back the next day, ready to do it all again.

From an early childhood perspective, those days taught us that meltdowns aren't solved by quick fixes, but by calm, steady support. One teacher comforting the most upset child. Another redirecting the group with bubbles or a song. A Director stepping in to help with paperwork. And always, always, a floater ready to jump in. Pro tip: you can never have too many floaters.

**

If drop-off was where love, chaos, and community collided at the classroom door, then the bigger picture of each school's personality showed up in how each location carried its own spirit. Even though all three schools shared the same heart, values, and culture, they were far from carbon copies of each other. They were like three siblings in the same family—clearly related, sharing DNA—but each with their own quirks, strengths, and character.

School #1 was our cozy, bustling pioneer. Tucked away in a commercial area, it had a scrappy, vibrant spirit, almost like a favorite neighborhood café where everyone knows your name. It was where everything started, the place of "firsts," where we built from scratch and figured things out step by step. That scrappy magic of our beginnings will always live there.

School #2 was our spacious, energetic hub. Right on a main road, it was designed for growth and scale. Its vibe felt more like a thriving campus, polished and busy, where systems and structure really mattered. It was here that we learned the importance of running a well-oiled machine, while still holding tight to the warmth and heart that defined us from the beginning.

School #3 was our deeply rooted community gem. Nestled right inside a master-planned neighborhood, it didn't just serve families. It belonged to them. It carried a spirit that felt less like a school and more like an extension of home. The loyalty of those parents, their pride in "their" school, and the way it became part of the fabric of their daily lives made its personality completely unique.

But beyond their personalities, each campus seemed to attract its own brand of funny moments and challenges. My Directors like to joke that the real variable wasn't the location, it was me. Wherever I showed up, the funny incidents seemed to follow. And honestly, they're not wrong.

Every morning, I made it a point to walk into each classroom and greet every teacher and every child. It became my ritual. The teachers teased me about it, because the minute I walked in, their carefully managed morning routines went out the window. The kids would mob me like I was Taylor Swift, shouting over one another to tell me about their weekend, showing me their artwork, or tugging on my arm to share stories about their new puppy or how they finally swam without floaties. The teachers would roll their eyes and laugh, pretending to be exasperated, but I knew deep down they loved it too. I sure did. I soaked up every single hug and story.

That said, each school had its own unique flavor of daily comedy and chaos, shaped by its location, its building, and the rhythm of the families around it. Take School #1, for example. Every morning, we had what I lovingly called the "Parking Lot Olympics." Because of its tight commercial location, parking was a daily adventure. Parents became experts at parallel parking on the fly, jogging across the lot with kids in one arm and three bags in the other. Watching it unfold every morning was like having front row seats to a sitcom. Exhausting for them, but endlessly entertaining from our windows.

The kids themselves, though, were the great equalizers. Toddlers are toddlers, no matter the zip code. They bring their humor, their honesty, and their chaos with them wherever they go. What made the real difference was the teachers. Some were naturally more serious and ran very structured, orderly classrooms with almost no behavior

75

issues. Others leaned into the joyful messiness of preschool life, allowing children's personalities to shine big and bright.

That's the style Ms. Annie, my Executive Director, and I always gravitated toward. The teachers who encouraged kids to truly be themselves. If a child loved art, we let them explore it fully. If another loved science, we set up experiments and let their curiosity lead. If reading was their passion, we gave them more books and space to share stories. When kids were allowed to dive into what they loved, you could feel the energy shift. Magic happened. Language flowed, laughter echoed, conversations blossomed. Learning became so natural, it was woven into play, and teamwork wasn't something we forced. It was something that happened organically because the kids wanted to work together.

Each school, in its own way, became a stage for this kind of magic. The personalities of the campuses gave the backdrop, but it was always the children and the teachers who brought it to life. And watching that unfold, day after day, was the most rewarding part of the job.

***

Of course, no matter the personality of the school or the differences in each location, there were always those days that reminded us preschool life is anything but predictable. You could plan schedules, write policies, and prepare for the usual chaos, but then there were the "you'll never believe what happened" days. They usually started with one small hiccup and snowballed into a masterclass of controlled pandemonium.

One such day stands out in my memory as if it were yesterday. It began with a call-out from a teacher—not because she was sick, but because she was in love. Newly engaged, she announced she wanted to become a stay-at-home fiancée. Forever. We were still shaking our heads at that one when Mrs. Jones came rushing to the front office to let us know that Jolie, who had just been dropped off, had thrown up. We got her settled, but before we could catch our breath, another parent walked in demanding an apology from another mom for something "rude" that was said at a birthday party over the weekend. As I stood there trying to empathize but also gently explain that we weren't exactly in the business of mediating adult social drama, the phone rang. Saved by the bell.

The call turned out to be a potential parent, the kind who asks every detail and requires a long, patient conversation. While I was tied up on the phone, a teacher flagged me down. There was a tour family waiting in the lobby. The only catch? They spoke only Spanish. Since I don't, I quickly deputized the teacher, who was literally on her way to grab construction paper, to step in. "Give the tour, answer what you can, I'll join you as soon as I'm free," I told her. On top of that, I asked her to cover a potty break for a teacher in the infant room. Suddenly, she had become a tour guide, substitute infant teacher, and supply runner all at once. A real hero of the day.

Just when I thought the chaos had balanced itself out, Jolie reappeared, sick again. Given that her best friend Jayden had been out with a tummy bug the day before, we realized this might be spreading. We called Jolie's mom and started drafting a class-wide email to notify parents. In the middle of that, little Colton came shuffling in, clutching his teacher's hand, tears streaming down his face. His crisis? A scrape so tiny you could barely see it. But to him, it was monumental. We gave him TLC, a Scooby-Doo band-aid, and just like that, the tears dried up.

Meanwhile, the Spanish-speaking family returned from their tour with lots of questions about pricing. That's when we realized there'd been a mix-up. Our "tour guide" had shown them the toddler classroom, assuming the little one in their arms was the future student. When in fact they were there to ask about after-school care for their third grader. No wonder they looked so puzzled as to why their big kid would be lumped in with our two-year-olds. Back out they went, this time to the right annex classroom, just as my Director finally arrived. I could breathe again.

The afternoon rolled in peacefully until lunchtime when, as if on cue, a storm warning hit. Flash flooding, early school district closings, the works. We had to call an early dismissal, reroute buses, send urgent parent emails, and field nonstop phone calls. By the end of the day, the exhaustion was real, but every child went home safe, and that's always the measure of success.

The day was wild, but it also showed me what makes preschool leadership so unique. The Spanish-speaking family ended up enrolling, thanks to the teacher who rose to the occasion. Jolie was back at school within days, happy and healthy. And the newly engaged teacher? Well, the Hallmark movie life didn't pan out, and she eventually called back asking for her job. By then, of course, her position was filled.

Days like that used to make me want to step in everywhere at once, but over time, I learned an important leadership lesson: knowing when to step forward and when to step back. In the beginning, I thought being a leader meant being at the center of every problem. But as we grew, I realized true leadership is about empowering others to take ownership.

I trusted my Directors to handle the day-to-day. The teachers, the parents, the small fires that popped up constantly. I focused on the bigger picture: strategic growth, finances, and making sure the culture of love, safety, and excellence never wavered. That meant letting my Directors make decisions, even if they made mistakes. Mistakes were learning opportunities, and watching them grow into strong, confident leaders was one of the most rewarding parts of my journey.

It was a conscious shift: moving from the person with all the answers to the person who helped others find their own. And if there's anything preschool crisis days taught me, it's that leadership isn't about avoiding the chaos. It's about teaching others to handle it with grace, humor, and heart.

***

If the chaos days taught me about leadership, the everyday stories of our teachers reminded me why we were there in the first place. The culture of a school isn't built from handbooks or policies. It's shaped by the heart of the staff who show up every day, often going above and beyond in ways that leave you humbled.

One of those stories was Ms. Taylor, a toddler teacher with a boy in her class who spoke only Norwegian. Instead of letting the language barrier stand in the way, she decided to learn. She sat with his parents, picked up conversational phrases, and slowly began speaking to him in his own tongue. For that little boy, navigating a brand-new world, she built a bridge. It was a small act on her part, but to him, it was everything.

Then there was Ms. Avery. On our big, celebratory PJ Day, she noticed Maya standing apart, crying because she didn't have pajamas like the other kids. Without hesitation, Ms. Avery jumped in her car, drove to the nearest store, and came back with a pair of unicorn PJs. Maya's face lit up with joy, and she spent the rest of the day twirling in them like she was the happiest girl alive. That's the kind of thing you don't forget.

But perhaps the most memorable story came from our Director, Ms. Ellianne. She was closing one evening when she noticed Lucas still hadn't been picked up. As time ticked down, she grew concerned. Calls to his parents went unanswered until finally, his mom, who was out of town, called back in a panic. It turned out that it was part of a divorce custody schedule, and dad had simply forgotten. It was his pickup day, but between work and a conference, he lost track. Without complaint, Ms. Ellianne and another teacher stayed with Lucas two hours after our school closed, until his dad arrived to receive him, making sure he felt safe and cared for the whole time. It was a reminder that sometimes life outside the school gets messy, and when it does, we step in. Not just as teachers, but as an extension of family.

Of course, not every memorable staff story was heavy. Laughter was part of our survival, and humor was what kept us strong. Like the time a surprise inspection caught us off guard. I gave what I thought was a clever, under-the-radar warning: "The eagle has landed." To me, it was a simple Apollo 11 reference. To one of our younger teachers, though, it meant we had an *actual eagle* arriving at the petting zoo. She spread the word quickly, and soon kids were running around excitedly asking, "Where's the eagle? Can we pet it?" The look on their faces when they realized there was no eagle. Just a clipboard-carrying licensing rep. It was priceless. From then on, anytime an inspector showed up, the staff would grin at me and whisper, "Petting zoo time!"

And then there was the legendary prank we pulled on Annie, our Executive Director. She'd been away on vacation, and when she returned, we convinced her that a huge Hollywood celebrity who grew up in our town had toured our school looking for an infant spot. We added every ridiculous detail we could: bodyguards, autograph signing, even a photo-shopped selfie. Annie, who adored celebrity gossip, ate up every word. She asked a hundred questions, completely convinced, even telling her dad. Who was a preacher! Months later, when she was still talking about it, we finally broke the news. Her reaction? "You made me lie to a preacher!" she said, half-scolding, half-laughing, before dissolving into giggles with the rest of us. That prank became part of our school lore, told again and again whenever someone needed a laugh.

But in between the pranks and the chaos were the celebrations that really mattered. We didn't wait for big events to recognize each other's hard work. Wins were celebrated in the moment, especially on tough days. A whispered, "You handled that beautifully," after a rough transition. A round of high-fives when a class mastered a new song. Or a surprise box of donuts in the breakroom after a morning that tested everyone's patience. Food, laughter, and small gestures were our love language. They were how we reminded one another that we were in this together.

At the end of the day, it wasn't just about curriculum or checklists. It was about people. Teachers who became heroes in a child's story. Teams who carried each other through long, messy days. And the quiet, consistent celebrations of each other that made our schools not just workplaces, but families.

＊

If the dedication of our teachers defined our culture, then the logic of our children defined our daily laughter.

Their way of seeing the world was refreshing, unexpected, and often left us shaking our heads in disbelief. Just when I thought I had seen it all, a child would say or do something that reminded me why working with preschoolers is equal parts heart and comedy.

One afternoon during free play, I noticed Kamryn with a sticky spot on her cheek. "Kamryn, what's on your face?" I asked. She shook her head with such seriousness that I knew she wasn't about to give me an answer. A moment later, I spotted Jackson with the same sticky smudge on his hand, and then Avery with one on his forehead. Clearly, something was going on. When I finally pressed them, Addison, who had been playing quietly at the sensory table, looked up with wide eyes and said, "It's the magic dust. It makes us invisible!" Turns out the "magic dust" was nothing more than a mixture of spilled glitter and applesauce. Not the invisibility potion they believed in—but magical enough to them.

Another day, a game of hide-and-seek spiraled into its own kind of comedy. Asma always hid in the treehouse, her shoes sticking out and her giggles giving her away. Julio and Bailey decided to cram in too, whispering loudly back and forth about who had the spot first. From behind the treehouse, Asma finally sighed, "Are you two having a party in there?" What began as a hiding game turned into an argument over who was "better," girls or boys, until the teacher playing seeker finally threw up her hands and said, "You all win!"

Then there was Kennedy, playing doctor with Ryker as her patient. With a toy stethoscope pressed to his chest, she announced with grave authority, "Hmm, your heart is making a lot of noise. It's too fast." Ryker, without missing a beat, explained, "I ran really fast! I was being a race car!" Kennedy shook her head. "No, you're just being loud. I need to give you a shot." She jabbed him with a toy syringe, and Ryker let out the most dramatic "Ouch!" you've ever heard.

Potty training brought its own kind of humor. One little boy was convinced the toilet was magical. After sitting there for ages, he proudly emerged and declared, "I did it! I made a puddle!" The "puddle," of course, was just water from the faucet. His teacher, Ms. Amy, tried to explain, "It's for when you have to go to the bathroom." He looked at her, puzzled. "But I did! I made a puddle!" Thinking quickly, she told him, "It's a different kind of puddle. A special puddle." He grinned mischievously. "Can I make another special puddle?" And off he ran, excited for another round.

Even naptime could take unexpected turns. Sammy, usually a solid sleeper, declared one afternoon, "I'm not tired! I'm a superhero!" Naturally, Valeria chimed in with, "I'm a princess! Princesses don't sleep!" and Christian joined, "I'm a race car! Race cars don't sleep!" Before long, the entire room was buzzing with superheroes, royalty, and vehicles that had no interest in resting. The teachers, in a stroke of brilliance, began telling a story about a superhero so tired from saving the world that he had to take a nap. Within minutes, the room was silent again, every last superhero and princess asleep.

And then there was the day Savannah and Payton were hard at work in the kitchen center. With all the seriousness of master chefs, they stirred imaginary concoctions in little teacups. Savannah finally presented hers with great pride. "Here you go!" she announced to Payton. Curious, I asked, "That looks delicious. What did you make?" Without missing a beat, Savannah puffed out her chest and declared, "Margaritas!" I almost choked holding back laughter. Payton, unfazed, took a big pretend sip. "Yummy!"

Moments like these reminded me daily of the beauty in children's logic. They saw the world through lenses unclouded by reason or convention, and in that freedom, they found endless possibilities.

Chapter 5: The Art Of The Tantrum (And Other Dramatic Performances)

If there's one thing I've learned from running a preschool, it's this: Broadway has nothing on a group of toddlers in full meltdown mode. Forget Shakespearean soliloquies—nothing tugs at the heartstrings (or frays the nerves) quite like a three-year-old who has just been handed the wrong color cup.

One child once threw a full-on Oscar-worthy tantrum in the middle of circle time because another child "stole her spot on the carpet"—even though there were twenty others available.

She dramatically threw herself down, sobbing into her little backpack, and when I asked what we could do to fix it, she wailed, "Only a unicorn hug will help me now!"

A teacher gently offered a unicorn plush from the reading nook, and wouldn't you know it... the healing began.

Tantrums, while exhausting, are an art form in themselves. The sheer range of emotions, the commitment to the scene, the way a child can go from full-body despair to cheerful giggles in a matter of seconds—it's truly impressive. And, as any seasoned early childhood educator will tell you, there's a certain beat to these dramatic performances.

For anyone who spends time with young children, they're an everyday reality. They can feel like big storms rolling through the classroom, but really, they're just signs of where a child is in their growth. Once you've been around them long enough, you start to notice the patterns, and it makes them easier to handle with a bit more patience (and sometimes a laugh).

In the end, it often comes down to just a few familiar triggers.

The first is *sharing*. This is the "mine!" stage, and it is very real. If another child so much as touches a favorite toy, a full-blown meltdown can follow. During toddler tours, I used to laugh with parents and say, "Once your child learns to say 'NO!' and 'MINE!'… your life is over!" And truly, it does feel that way sometimes.

Then there's *independence.* Toddlers want to do everything themselves. Pour their own juice, put on their shoes, pick their activities. If you step in to help, even kindly, it can feel like the end of the world to them. My advice to parents was always, if they can do it, or are eager to try, let them.

Transitions are another tough spot. Imagine working hard on the tallest block tower of your life and then being told to put it away. That's a lot to ask of a three-year-old!

Teachers quickly learn the power of songs and routines to make moving on feel fun instead of frustrating.

And, of course, we can't forget *basic needs*. Hunger, tiredness, or being overstimulated can all flip a switch. I know this well from raising my boys. When they were little, the park was our second home, and later it was basketball courts and baseball fields. Sometimes the best way to avoid meltdowns is just to let them run, play, and get the wiggles out.

The last big one is *communication*. Younger children often know what they want but don't yet have the words. Their frustration comes out in crying, shouting, or hitting. One simple trick is to give them the words yourself: "I can see that you're sad because Neil didn't want to play soccer with you." It helps them start to connect their feelings with language.

Still, not all emotional episodes look the same. Toddlers (ages one to three) are usually crying out of pure frustration. They don't have the words yet, and it all comes spilling out in tears and kicks. Preschoolers (ages three to five), on the other hand, know how to talk and sometimes use these big feelings as a way to push limits or bargain.

***

I'll never forget Elvin, who had just turned two. He adored trains. One morning, he was trying to push a square block into a round hole on the train table. He tried once, then again, grunting with effort. On the third try, when it still didn't fit, he threw the block across the room and collapsed on the floor in a heap, kicking and sobbing. He never even said a word. Just pure, overwhelming frustration. His teacher, Ms. Anna, didn't try to fix it. She just sat nearby with a calm hand and let him ride it out. Sometimes, that's all they need.

Now compare that to Brooklyn, who was four. She wanted to be line leader, again. But it was Aileen's turn. Brooklyn planted her hands on her hips and pouted, "But I wanna be the line leader!" When her teacher reminded her it was someone else's turn and offered her the job of door holder instead, Brooklyn gasped like she'd been deeply wronged. "No! If I can't be line leader, I'm never lining up again. Ever!" And when that didn't work, she switched gears. She started wailing for her mommy, who wasn't coming for another hour. It wasn't raw despair like Elvin. It was strategy, testing to see if drama could change the rules.

Certain parts of the day are tantrum hot spots. Morning drop-off is a big one—separating from mom or dad is hard, even for kids who love school. Before lunch is another, when kids are hungry and their patience is gone. Naptime can be a battle of wills, because no one wants to miss out on the fun. And at the end of the day, believe it or not, some kids cry because they don't want to leave.

The truth is, these flare-ups don't just show up out of nowhere. They follow cycles, needs, and stages. Once you understand that, you stop seeing them as pure chaos and start seeing them for what they are: kids learning how to be human. And yes, they test every ounce of patience we have, but they also teach us so much along the way.

It always starts small. A furrowed brow. A deep sigh. A dramatic slouch. The seasoned teachers among us can sense it coming before it even begins.

Take Lucas, for example. He was a sweet, happy-go-lucky kid, until it was time to line up for recess. Every day, without fail, he had to be first in line. If he wasn't? Well, that's when it got interesting. The lip would quiver, the arms would cross, and suddenly, we had a crisis on our hands.

"Lucas, buddy, you can be the line leader tomorrow!" I'd say cheerfully. "We have to take turns and give our friends an opportunity".

"But I want to be it now!" he'd wail, stomping his tiny foot with all the power his 35-pound frame could muster.

Cue the deep breath. The furrowed brow. The dramatic collapse onto the floor. Ladies and gentlemen, we had officially entered…the tantrum stage!

The full-blown tantrum has many variations, from the silent, lip-trembling devastation to the all-out, limbs-flailing-on-the-floor spectacle.

I'll never forget Madison, the reigning queen of the "silent protest." She wouldn't scream, cry, or even speak. Instead, she'd lock eyes with me, lower herself very slowly to the ground, and just... lie there. Completely motionless. For minutes on end.

Meanwhile, across the room, Jackson specialized in the dramatic escape. If something didn't go his way, he wouldn't just cry—he'd attempt a full-on jailbreak. More than once, I found my teachers jogging across the playground to gently redirect him back inside, all while he declared, "I'm never coming back!"

And then, of course, there was Ella, a true artist in the medium of theatrical sobbing. She didn't just cry—she wept, complete with gasping breaths and poetic proclamations of injustice.

"Ms. Ashli," she once wailed, clutching my hand, "I can never be happy again because I didn't get the purple marker!"

I nodded solemnly. "That's really hard."

She sniffled. "I know."

Five minutes later, she was laughing with her friends, completely over it.

If you spend enough time in preschool, you start to notice that these crying spells aren't just random outbursts. They're performances, and every child has their own signature style. The reasons might change from day to day, but the delivery? Oh, that becomes as familiar as a favorite TV rerun. It's almost like kids fall into their own "tantrum personalities," and once you've seen a few, you can spot them a mile away.

We've already met the dramatic sobbers and the silent protesters, but there are plenty more to add to the cast.

Take *The Negotiator*. This child could hold their own in a courtroom. Their tantrum isn't just about crying. It's about bargaining. It usually starts with a demand, quickly escalates to a threat ("If I don't get the blue car, I'm never eating my lunch!"), and then spirals into more and more creative deals. They're not interested in compromise; they're out for a total win. In their little world, there's no such thing as "let's meet halfway." There's only "I get my way, or the world ends."

Then there's *The Melancholy Mime*, or as I like to call them, the "Melly Nellys." This is the child who doesn't bother with loud wails. Instead, they just collapse dramatically onto the floor, face down, cheeks pressed to the tile, looking like a heartbroken Saint Bernard. No words, no explanations. Just a slumped little body radiating pure despair. The performance is designed to pull at your heartstrings, and let me tell you, it works. It's silent, but oh, so powerful.

Another classic is *The Human Anomaly*. These are the ones that catch you completely off guard. Their meltdowns aren't about toys, or sharing, or even naps. No, these are about things no adult could ever predict. Their socks feel funny. The sun is too bright. Their name has too many letters. I once had a child scream because the sky was the "wrong shade of blue." There's no reasoning here, because the reasoning belongs to a toddler's universe. And trust me, that universe plays by very different rules.

And finally, there's *The All-in Actor*. This child is committed. Every ounce of their little body is thrown into the performance. Tears, sighs, flailing limbs, even dramatic moans. It's a full-body spectacle that sometimes combines all the other archetypes in one. Watching one of these meltdowns is like seeing a toddler put on their very own Broadway show. Exhausting, yes, but you have to admire the dedication.

Teachers go through hours and hours of professional development with titles like "behavior management," "classroom management," or "social and emotional learning." I've hosted plenty of these myself, and while the names sound official and important, the real magic doesn't happen in the training room. It happens on the floor of a classroom, in the middle of the noise and chaos, when a teacher has to figure out how to bring a child back from the edge without making a big announcement about what "technique" they're about to use.

Over the years, we've collected an arsenal of tricks. Silly, memorable, but very effective. They aren't the polished, textbook strategies you find in a binder. They're the battle-tested, passed-down methods that parents and teachers swap like secrets in the hallway.

Here are a few of my favorites:

1. The "Squirrel" Technique: This one never fails. When two children are in a tug-of-war over a toy, the teacher simply takes the toy out of the equation and creates a sudden distraction. "Oh wow, is that a plane in the sky?" or "Look at that bug on the window!" The surprise is usually enough to break the spell.

2. The "Human Blanket" Method: For the full-body meltdowns, when a child collapses on the floor in despair, sometimes the best thing is to sit quietly beside them. No reasoning, no scolding, just a calm presence and maybe a hug when they're ready. Your body becomes the anchor in their storm.

3. The "Morgan Freeman Documentary" Strategy: This is one of my favorites. You narrate the child's feelings calmly, almost like a voiceover. "It looks like you're feeling really mad because your block tower fell down. I know you worked so hard on it." It gives their big emotions words and lets them know you see them.

4. The "Magic Eraser" Approach: For the tantrums that make no sense to anyone but the child, you bring in a little magic. "Oh no, you wanted triangles instead of squares? Let's use my magic finger to fix it!" A playful tap can turn a sandwich into "triangles," and suddenly the tears stop.

5. The "Time-Traveler" Trick: When a child is stuck wanting something they can't have, you gently shift their focus forward. "I know you want another turn on the slide, but after nap, we're going to read your favorite book. What do you think happens next in the

story?" Sometimes hope for later is enough to calm the now.

6. The "Tiny Diplomat" Protocol: When two kids are arguing, we bring them into a mini negotiation. "Justin, it's Kyle's turn with the red car. What can you say to Kyle for a turn?" Using "I feel" statements and teaching them the language of compromise makes the whole moment feel like a tiny peace summit.

7. The "Librarian": This one is powerful for loud meltdowns. Instead of raising your own voice, you do the opposite. You whisper. "I can't hear you when you're shouting. I can listen when you use your quiet voice." And little by little, the child lowers their voice so they can hear you.

The truth is, the very best tantrum strategy is prevention. Teachers learn to put out the sparks before they become a fire. That means walking into a room with confidence, setting clear expectations, and giving kids a sense of ownership in what they're doing. Children are emotional barometers. They know if you're unsure or nervous. But when you're calm, steady, and in charge, they feel safe.

Consistency is just as important. Kids need the same rules to apply every day. If "walking feet" is a rule one day and not the next, that's an open invitation to a power struggle. Predictability gives them security.

And then, there's the magic of buy-in. Instead of ordering a child to clean up, you might say, "Let's put the red blocks in the red bin. Can you find the first one?" Suddenly, it's teamwork, not a demand.

Even snack time can be smoothed out with a little choice. If you ask, "What do you want for snack?" you're inviting a meltdown when the answer is "cupcakes." But if you ask, "Would you like a banana or an apple?" they feel powerful choosing, and you're still in control of the options.

At the end of the day, all of these tricks come down to the same thing: staying calm, being consistent, and remembering that a tantrum isn't a power play—it's a little person trying to figure out big feelings in a big world.

Of course, every so often, you get a child who adds a little *creativity* to the mix. And honestly? Those are the moments that keep us laughing for years.

I used to joke that kids are smarter than adults, and sometimes they prove it. My son Parker, for instance, was a born negotiator. His meltdowns weren't about losing control; they were about making a deal. He'd come up to me with this half-smile, half-smirk, and start with, "Mom, do I have a deal for you!" One sunny day, he wanted to wear his winter boots. When I told him it was too warm, he didn't collapse in despair. Instead, he counter-offered: "If I don't wear my winter boots today, can I have a bag of candy?" I had to laugh. The kid knew how to bargain.

His brother Pierce was completely different. He never cared to win the fight. He cared to make it funny. If he was upset, he'd find a way to turn it into a game or a laugh, and before you knew it, the tantrum had disappeared in a puff of silliness.

And then there was Preston, my stubborn, alligator-teared one. Once he dug in his heels, there was no negotiating, no distraction, no turning back. His outbursts were pure, raw storm clouds that just had to pass. Only after the storm cleared could you reason with him.

Those moments of unexpected creativity, whether a clever bargain, a joke, or a full-force meltdown, are the ones that stick with you. They remind me that these kids aren't just little people; they're brilliant, baffling, hilarious individuals trying to make sense of the world in their own way. And for all the chaos and noise, I wouldn't trade it for all the money in Fort Knox.

And of course, sometimes that creativity becomes the tantrum itself. Which brings us to one of the most familiar acts of all, the negotiation.

***

What's most fascinating about these dramatic displays is that, despite the level of distress a child seems to be experiencing, they can be surprisingly strategic when it comes to getting what they want.

I once had a little boy named Sebastian who, in the middle of a dramatic outburst over snack time, paused mid-sob and whispered, "Ms. Ashli... what if I only have one extra cookie? Just one. Then I'll stop crying."

Nice try, kid.

Teachers quickly become masters of de-escalation, learning when to offer comfort, when to distract, and when to just let the storm pass. The key is patience—and a good sense of humor.

One time, after a particularly exhausting morning, I sat down with a cup of coffee only to have a three-year-old crawl into my lap, sigh deeply, and say, "Ugh, kids are so dramatic."

Yes. Yes, they are.

***

The thing about tantrums is they almost always end just as suddenly as they begin. One minute, a child is inconsolable, the next, they're happily building a block tower as if nothing ever happened.

It's the emotional whiplash that really gets you.

I once had a little girl scream for ten full minutes because she didn't want to wear her coat outside. Then, as soon as we stepped onto the playground, she turned to me, beaming, and said, "I love my coat! It's so pretty!"

I just stared at her, wondering if I had imagined the past ten minutes.

And that's the magic (and madness) of early childhood.

One of my favorites involves two three-year-old best friends. They got into what can only be described as a world-shaking argument because they both thought only one person was allowed to like Elsa. The tears weren't just ordinary crying; they were the full-body kind, shoulders shaking and faces blotchy. "But I like Elsa!" one of them wailed, only to be met with, "No, I like Elsa!" from the other. To them, it wasn't just a disagreement—it was a battle for the sole right to adore a Disney princess. The teachers sat them down and explained that millions of people all over the world loved Elsa at the same time. Instead of relief, this revelation led to a fresh round of tears. The injustice of shared affection was too much to bear.

I also have to include one from home. My son Parker once gave me a meltdown so legendary that it has stayed with me ever since. We were driving, and out of nowhere, from the backseat, he screamed in fury, "He's looking out MY window!" His brother Preston had dared to look out the wrong side of the car. Parker's face was red with righteous anger, as if Preston had stolen his birthright. I had to bite my lip to keep from laughing, because what kind of crime is looking out of someone else's window? But to Parker, it was the ultimate betrayal.

Then there was the mysterious tantrum of the green cup. A boy came to his teacher, lip trembling, and requested water in his green cup. She kindly filled it and handed it back to him. He looked at the cup, then let out a scream so primal you'd think we'd handed him a rattlesnake. He fell to the floor, thrashing and sobbing. No one could figure it out. He had asked for the green cup. He had water in the green cup. And yet, his world was over. It was one of those moments where you just shake your head, because sometimes the logic is beyond us.

Another child arrived at school one morning already heartbroken. Her best friend was beaming and telling the class it was her birthday. Instead of celebrating with her, the first girl crumbled into sobs. Through her tears she managed to explain, "She's my best friend! We're supposed to have the same birthday!" The discovery that life hadn't aligned their birth dates was too much. She had to be comforted in the quiet corner, the weight of this cosmic betrayal too heavy for her little shoulders.

And finally, the one that makes everyone laugh every time it's retold. A little boy sat happily at the table when a small noise escaped him. He had farted. His smile immediately vanished, his face crumpled, and he began to wail in absolute devastation. When I asked what was wrong, he sobbed, "I was saving that for later!" There it was. The heartbreak of a wasted fart. It's the kind of thing you couldn't make up if you tried.

These are the stories that we teachers swap over coffee, dinner, or even a well-earned glass of wine. They're the ones that remind us why the job is exhausting and hilarious all at once. And yes, sometimes the only way to get through a tantrum is to hide your laughter until it's safe to let it out.

As exhausting as they are, these meltdowns serve an important purpose. They teach children how to navigate their emotions, how to handle disappointment, and how to eventually express their frustrations in a more productive way.

For us teachers, they're a lesson in patience, empathy, and flexibility. They remind us that kids don't have the emotional regulation skills that adults do (and let's be honest—some adults don't have them either).

But most of all, they provide us with some of the best, funniest, and most unforgettable stories.

Because at the end of the day, preschool isn't just about being prepared for Kindergarten—it's about learning how to be human. And sometimes, that means throwing yourself onto the floor over a missing crayon.

And honestly? I kind of get it.

Chapter 6: Creative Chaos—
Masterpieces And Mayhem

If you ever want to witness true artistic passion, forget the Louvre or the Met—just step into a preschool art room. Here, creativity runs wild, and the rules of traditional art don't apply. A purple sky? Sure. A dog with five legs? Why not? A self-portrait that looks more like a blob with spaghetti arms? Pure genius.

Art time in a preschool is a sacred event—an opportunity for tiny hands to transform paper, paint, glue, and an alarming amount of glitter into something they are convinced belongs in a museum. The only downside? The absolute chaos that ensues.

Every teacher knows that art time is a delicate dance. You want to encourage free expression, but you also want to make it out alive without a child glueing their shirt to the table.

I learned this the hard way.

During one of our first big "creative days," I had this grand idea: Let's do a full-body tracing project. Each child would lay on a giant sheet of paper, we'd trace their outline, and they'd decorate it however they wanted. Simple, right?

Wrong.

Within minutes:

Aiden had wrapped himself in tape like a mummy.

Abigail was rolling in paint like a miniature Jackson Pollock.

Someone (I still don't know who) managed to get glue on the ceiling.

And three kids had somehow cut their drawings into "puzzle pieces" and were sobbing because they "broke" themselves.

Lesson learned: Never underestimate the destructive potential of children armed with craft supplies.

***

In most preschools, the idea of having one big, beautiful "art room" sounds amazing, but it's not very practical, especially when you're running on the kind of budget that owners like me usually have. Space is precious. So instead, our preschools had art centers inside every classroom. Each one was like a tiny, self-contained world of creativity.

Before the children arrived, those little corners had a magic to them. The smell of fresh clay, clean paper, and tempera paint filled the air. Paint bottles were lined up in rows, paper was stacked neatly in piles, and little bins held brushes, glue sticks, and scraps of colorful paper. It looked calm, organized, and almost too perfect.

Of course, this was only the morning version. By the end of the day, it was another story. Supplies were scattered, brushes were soaking, and paper scraps seemed to multiply on their own. It wasn't messy in a bad way. It was the kind of mess that meant creativity had happened. A smudge of paint on a smock, a half-finished collage on the table, a bit of clay left behind, all proof that something had been created and shared. The art centers were alive with children's voices, asking questions, sharing supplies, and encouraging each other. To me, those "creative catastrophes" were the best evidence of learning.

And here's the thing: as adults, we often want children's art to look "just right." We want pumpkins to be orange, skies to be blue, and clothes to stay clean. But in a preschool, real art is messy. That's why we put children in oversized t-shirts, aprons, or smocks. It was our way of saying, "Go ahead, get messy. The process matters more than the product." A blue pumpkin might not make sense to us, but it makes perfect sense to the child who drew it. Art is their way of showing us what's going on inside their minds, and we can't put limits on that.

Art gives children so much more than just a finished picture to take home. It helps them with:

- Emotional regulation: A child who is too upset to find words can scribble or paint to release those big feelings.
- Social skills: Working together on a project means learning to share, take turns, and talk through ideas.
- Confidence: Every drawing, painting, or sculpture is a statement of "I made this." That sense of pride carries into every part of their life.
- Physical and cognitive growth: Holding crayons, cutting paper, shaping clay. These aren't just fun, they're building fine motor skills and coordination. Even talking about their art builds language skills.

The greatest gift we could give our children wasn't a perfect art center. It was the freedom to be messy, to explore, and to create whatever came to mind.

Now, when it came to introducing art projects, we had our own little ritual. We simply called it "Creative Art." If you went to a professional training, you'd probably hear it described with fancy terms like *child-led art* or *narrative art.* But for us, it was simply this: we gave the children a variety of materials and asked them to tell us a story with their creations.

It wasn't about handing out pumpkin worksheets and saying, "Use orange." Instead, a teacher might gather the children and say, "Halloween is coming up. What does Halloween mean to you? What do you hope to create today? What colors will you use?" And off they would go. Some drew pumpkins in blue, some drew their costumes, others made ghosts that looked more silly than spooky. Once, a little girl even drew a slide because, for her, Halloween meant going down the slide at the school carnival. The teacher's role was never to dictate but to guide, to encourage their ideas and let their imaginations lead the way.

And imagination isn't limited to crayons and markers. Some of the best projects came from the most unexpected supplies. We've used:

- Potato stamps. Ms. Jaime once brought in potatoes and carved them into shapes. The kids stamped out stars, hearts, and even little elephants.
- Nature items. Ms. Dina would take the children on walks to collect leaves, sticks, feathers, and pinecones. Back in the classroom, they turned them into collages full of texture.
- Bubble wrap. Instead of throwing it away, we dipped it in paint and pressed it onto paper to make bubbly textures.
- Shaving cream. Spread on a table, it became a fun, sensory-rich medium for finger painting.
- Buttons. Old jars of buttons were turned into patterns and sculptures.
- Yarn and glue. A simple ball of yarn transformed into colorful, tangled designs.
- Dried pasta. Penne, rotini, and bow-tie pasta became mosaics and 3D art.

Those kinds of supplies reminded us that art really is everywhere. And sometimes, the most beautiful creations come from the simplest things.

The best stories come from the moments when things go completely off the rails. And yes, we've had plenty of those. Some were so messy they made a glitter spill look like nothing.

One that comes to mind was our big plan to make nature collages. The children had gone on a walk and collected pinecones, sticks, and leaves. The idea was simple: glue everything onto cardboard. Easy, right? Not with liquid glue and three-year-olds. Within minutes, glue was everywhere. On the tables, in hair, on clothes, and on little hands stuck to each other. The pinecones refused to stay in place, and one little boy, fed up, hurled his pinecone straight at the wall. There it stayed, like a sticky little monument to his frustration. Poor Ms. Christina stood there with glue on her hands, sighed, and said with the driest humor, "Okay, team, we are going to pivot. The glue has decided to be the art project today. Let's just draw with crayons!" And just like that, the Great Pinecone Disaster came to an end.

Then there was the "paintcano eruption." We had those giant gallon jugs of tempera paint, and during one busy morning, a child ran right into the art cart. The jug tipped, the lid flew off, and suddenly a wave of bright blue paint came gushing out like a river. It splattered on the floor, on the walls, on the children. One big blue explosion. Somehow it even reached the ceiling. The children stood frozen, staring wide-eyed, while I just thought, "This is it. I'll be repainting this whole classroom floor." For the rest of the day, the kids walked around with smurf-blue hands and faces, giggling every time they caught sight of each other. And to this day, there's still a faint blue stain on the ceiling that no mop could touch.

Sometimes our projects went sideways, not because of a mess, but because the kids were too smart for our plans. Like the day Ms. Yasi decided to mix art with cooking. The children made pudding, chocolate and vanilla, and the idea was to "paint" with their edible creations. For about two minutes, it went beautifully. Then one child (not Parker this time!) picked up their cup of pudding and simply ate it. That was all it took. Like dominoes falling, the whole class followed. Some daintily licked fingers, others licked pudding straight off their papers, and one little girl even chewed on her shirt where a drop had landed. I happened to be giving a tour to new parents that very moment. Through the observation window, the dad looked delighted, the mom looked horrified, and poor Ms. Yasi looked at me with a silent apology. I could only shrug. Just then, I saw Zoe lean in and lick pudding off her friend's cheek, and I thought, "Well, that's it. Pudding art is officially retired." Needless to say, that was both the first and last time we ever used pudding as paint.

Another time, we tried to make homemade kinetic sand with the kids. The recipe was supposed to be easy. Sand, cornstarch, and water. What we got instead was a gritty, sticky sludge that stuck to everything. It clumped into hair, smeared onto clothes, and glued itself to the floor like it had moved in for good. Every attempt to sweep it just spread the mess further. Eventually, we gave up and scraped it off in chunks. It was definitely a sensory experience, just not the one we had planned.

One of my personal favorites, though, was our straw painting project. The plan was simple: put drops of watery paint on paper, and the kids would blow through straws to spread the colors. At first, it worked beautifully. Then a few kids decided to see how hard they could blow. Paint started shooting everywhere. Splattering across the tables, flying onto easels, and spraying onto the kids sitting nearby. And because preschoolers are preschoolers, it quickly turned into a competition to see who could blow the hardest. Before we knew it, some children had inhaled paint, sticking out their tongues with rainbow stains, while others were laughing so hard they could barely breathe. The artwork looked nothing like what we'd imagined, but the room was full of giggles, colored splatters, and joy. And honestly, that was better than any finished product we could have planned.

***

Preschoolers have an interesting relationship with their artwork. Some are perfectionists, agonizing over every detail. Others take a more... let's say, "abstract" approach.

One of the things we looked forward to each year was our annual Art Auction. We framed the children's artwork, set up a gallery walk, and invited parents to "bid" on their child's creation. All proceeds went to charity. Let's be real—who's going to say no to their child's glitter-splashed masterpiece? We raised thousands of dollars for incredible causes this way, and the pride on the children's faces as their artwork was "sold" was priceless.

We also had our very own Art Car Parade—preschool style. Each class decorated wagons and trikes with streamers, recycled cardboard, and whatever shiny objects they could get their hands on. Firetrucks, Ambulances, Superhero getaway vehicles, Transformers, and even a few questionable transportation vehicles... we had it all! We paraded through the parking lot like royalty. Parents showed up with cameras, teachers wore funny hats, and the kids thought they were celebrities. It was chaotic and colorful and absolutely unforgettable.

Take Mason, as another example. Mason loved to draw. Every day, without fail, he'd present me with a new "masterpiece," which usually consisted of a giant scribble in one color. I'd say, "Wow, Mason! Tell me about your drawing!"

Without missing a beat, he'd reply, "It's a dragon eating a taco."

Of course it was.

Then there was Olivia, who refused to believe that her drawing wasn't real. One day, after painting a picture of a butterfly, she tried to set it free outside. When it didn't fly away, she burst into tears. "Ms. Ashli, she's stuck!" she wailed.

Cue me scrambling to explain the difference between real butterflies and painted butterflies while also admiring the depth of her belief in her own artistic abilities.

**

By now, you probably know how passionate I am about art centers. To me, they are little windows into the minds of tiny geniuses. While we, as adults, often look for realism or neatness, children are the true masters of narrative, surrealism, and sometimes hilariously brutal honesty. Their work is a gallery of surprises that can stop you in your tracks.

I'll never forget a little boy named Harry who had a very specific style. While the other children were busy with stick figures and colorful scribbles, he was carefully drawing houses with a ruler. They were precise, with sharp roofs and lots of windows, but never any doors or people. When a parent once asked him what they were, he answered completely straight-faced, "Houses for the sun." It was a perfectly logical answer in his world, and one of those moments that remind you how differently children see things.

Then there was Sofia, who had a knack for the surreal. One day, she showed me a chaotic, but beautiful painting of her family. Off to one side was a giant, angry-looking red scribble. She pointed to it and explained, "That's my dad when he runs on the running-machine." Of course, she meant the treadmill. It was hilarious, but also so real. She had captured the wild energy of her dad's workouts in a way only a child could.

Some pieces don't just surprise you with imagination, but with genuine skill. Chloe, one of the quietest girls in the class, once sat patiently with a ball of clay while the other children rolled out long "snakes." When she finally called me over, she held out the tiniest, most delicate little snail. It had a spiraled shell and even tiny ridges on its body. I was completely stunned. In that small, quiet moment, Chloe showed me that there is always so much more happening inside a child than we might ever guess.

And of course, there are the unintentionally funny masterpieces that become legends in our "Hall of Fame." One year, a boy named Richard proudly handed me a drawing. "This is my mom!" he said. The picture was a monster with six legs, huge teeth, and one giant eye. I asked him gently, "That's very creative, Richard! What do you love most about her?" He grinned and replied, "She's wearing her happy face!" I had to laugh. It was both terrifying and sweet at the same time.

Another unforgettable one happened on Father's Day. The classroom was buzzing with excitement as the kids worked on special artwork for their dads. Little Riley, grinning from ear to ear, ran to his teacher, Ms. Cora, with a drawing he couldn't wait to share. The picture… well, let's just say it looked a little *different* from an adult's perspective. A long shape, fire at the bottom, and a round part at the top. Ms. Cora tried to keep her composure and asked, "Tell me about your picture, Riley." Riley, proud as could be, declared, "It's my dad riding on a space shuttle! Zoom, zoom! He's going to the moon!" He even made rocket noises, pointing to the fire he had drawn.

Later, Riley's dad came in, smiling knowingly. "Riley showed me his drawing," he said with a wink. "Told me I was riding a very powerful space shuttle. Let's just say it was a memorable gift." We all laughed about it, and it quickly became one of those stories that lived on in our preschool archives.

***

There's a reason most teachers have a love-hate relationship with glitter, flitter, or any other form of it. While it adds sparkle and excitement to any project, it also never goes away. Ever.

Preschool teachers are the most creative humans on the planet. Give them a few empty paper towel rolls, a glue stick, and some googly eyes, and you'll get a functioning castle, complete with a moat. We made smocks from old t-shirts, turned pizza boxes into easels, and repurposed classroom clutter into craft gold.

It wasn't about having fancy supplies—it was about having heart, resourcefulness, and the ability to see magic in the everyday.

One day, I made the mistake of letting the kids use glitter without strict supervision. Within minutes, the room looked like a fairy godmother had sneezed all over it.

The best part? It wasn't just on the tables or the floors—it was everywhere. On hair, faces, and even in socks. One kid even had it in his ears.

Days later, I was still finding traces of glitter. I went to the grocery store, looked down at my hands, and realized I was still sparkling like a preschool disco ball.

I have no doubt that, somewhere in that classroom, there's still glitter embedded in the floorboards, waiting to resurface years from now.

***

Art time isn't just about self-expression—it's also prime time for some of the most passionate preschool debates.

Like the time two kids nearly came to blows over whether the sun should be yellow or green. (Spoiler: We compromised and made it rainbow.)

Or the time James insisted his drawing was of a "fire-breathing spaghetti monster," and his best friend Owen refused to accept this reality. "That's not a monster, James. That's just a scribble."

James, deeply offended, crossed his arms and declared, "Well, you don't know real art."

And thus, the preschool version of an art-world rivalry was born.

We cherished every finger-painted swirl and glitter-splashed canvas like it belonged in the Louvre and hung them on walls for display. The best part was watching parents try to decode the pieces.

I'll never forget one dad staring at his child's very… interpretive painting. He tilted his head left, then right, held it at arm's length, squinted, and finally said, "Wow! And… what is it?" The little artist beamed, "It's YOU, Daddy—when you're eating a cheeseburger!"

If this painting was displayed during our previously mentioned Art Auction, it would be sold to the slightly embarrassed dad in the second row.

Then there's the sheer volume of artwork that parents have to manage. Preschoolers don't just make one drawing a week—they produce dozens. By the end of the year, most parents could wallpaper their entire house with their child's masterpieces.

***

If you think the kids' art is entertaining, just wait until you see the parents' reactions. Teachers have seen it all, long before the internet, argued about whether a dress was blue and black or white and gold. Some parents laugh until they cry, others just cry, and a few even try to sneak their child's artwork right off the walls when they think no one is looking.

One year, there was a dad who looked like he could wrestle a bear and win. He was standing in front of his son's finger painting. Just an abstract splash of red, yellow, and blue. He stared at it for a long time, completely silent. Then one single tear rolled down his cheek. He turned to me and whispered, almost choked up, "He used his thumbprint. Right there. It's him. It's a tiny piece of him forever." It wasn't about the painting. It was about what it represented. To him, it was priceless.

Another mom stood in front of her daughter's collage of green yarn and brown paper. Her face lit up and she gasped, "Oh, that's our trip to the zoo last weekend!" In her eyes, the yarn was a snake and the brown paper was dirt. It wasn't just scraps of paper. It was a memory of love and connection.

And then there are the moments that are just plain funny. A dad once stood staring at his son's crayon drawing of a man with giant ears, a squished-up face, and a huge grin. "I don't get it," he muttered. His son ran up and proudly said, "That's you, Daddy! That's your laughy face!" The dad immediately burst out laughing. "Well, I guess that is what I look like!"

Sometimes, the parents' love for their child's art is so strong that they don't even care about the rules. To reinforce a monthly theme, we once created a giant mural in the foyer. A glorious mess of butcher paper, paint, and glued-on sticks. It was beautiful chaos. One dad thought I wasn't looking and tried to peel his son's piece right off the mural. When I caught him, he turned beet red and shoved his hands in his pockets with a guilty smile.

Another time, a mom saw her daughter's very first drawing of a face. A simple circle with two dots and a line. She burst into tears and begged me to let her take it home. I explained that we had to leave it up to show progress, but she returned the next day with a camera and took a photo of it. That was a moment of pure grace.

But sometimes, parents try to "interpret" their child's work… and let's just say, they don't always get it right. A mom once pointed to her daughter's abstract swirls of blue, white, and yellow and said, "Oh, this must be our trip to the beach!" Her daughter gave her a blank look and replied, "No, Mommy. That's a T-Rex trying to eat a banana." The mom froze, staring at the painting, clearly trying, and failing, to see it.

Another dad looked worried when he saw his son's drawing of a very grumpy face. "Are you mad at me, bud?" he asked. His son giggled and said, "No, Daddy. That's your face when you get a speeding ticket!"

And at our annual Art Auction, a mom stood admiring her son's lumpy brown clay sculpture. Smiling proudly, she said, "Is this a cup for flowers?" Her son patted it lovingly and replied, "No, Mommy. That's a dinosaur poop." The mom laughed so hard he nearly fell over.

The beauty of these moments is that parents, just like us, get to see their children's inner world. Whether it moves them to tears, makes them laugh until their stomachs hurt, or leaves them totally confused. Children's art is never just art. It's memory, meaning, and magic, all rolled into one.

***

Despite the chaos, the mess, and the occasional glitter-related trauma, creative time is one of the most important parts of early childhood education.

It teaches kids confidence. It teaches them problem-solving. It helps them express themselves in ways that words sometimes can't.

And, most importantly, it reminds us that art doesn't have to be perfect to be meaningful. Sometimes, the best masterpieces are the ones that make us laugh, make us wonder, or—at the very least—make us question how a child managed to glue their sock to the table.

And honestly? I wouldn't have it any other way.

But beyond the paintbrushes and googly eyes, there was so much real learning happening—quietly, joyfully, and sometimes in disguise. And contrary to the stories I have been sharing in pure spirit, our teachers were always in control, teaching, demonstrating, guiding, listening, asking, coaching, and learning from the kids. That's the magic of preschool: Learning is always happening!

Our curriculum was thoughtfully built around the belief that kids learn best when they're engaged, not just instructed. We followed a robust academic foundation rooted in hands-on, play-based learning using open-ended questions. There was a delicate balance of teacher-led and student-led activities. Yes, we taught letters and numbers, but we also taught how to ask questions, how to wonder out loud, how to try something new without being afraid of getting it wrong. By the time the students moved on to kindergarten, they were beyond ready with their knowledge and skills.

We had Career Day, where kids dressed up as veterinarians, chefs, astronauts, and engineers. And when they presented their "jobs" to the class, the pride in their voices and the light in their eyes told us everything we needed to know—they were dreaming big. And they believed in those dreams because we did too.

We had "Show-and-Tell"—where each child had the chance to stand up and speak in front of their peers, building confidence in ways that would serve them far beyond preschool. For some kids, just saying their name into a microphone was a huge leap. But the more they practiced, the taller they stood. And every round of applause made them feel seen and celebrated.

Our science center was always buzzing. One week we'd be making volcanoes erupt with baking soda and vinegar, the next we'd be growing plants in baggies taped to the windows. I'll never forget the day a group of four-year-olds "discovered" mold on a forgotten sandwich in a Ziploc bag during a food experiment. They were horrified—and then fascinated. "Can we name it?" one of them asked. (We did. His name was Larry.)

My favorite moments in the classroom happened when a child would ask me "Did you know..." questions. And for the record, if a child looks up at you all excited, asking you this question, No, you don't ever know. Then they would continue, "a melted snowball makes just a tiny puddle because most of the snow is actually air". No kid, I did not know that. Tell me more.

Even during the messiest days—mud pies on the playground, glitter explosions in the art room, or dramatic reenactments of fairy tales gone wildly off script—our students were learning. Learning how to negotiate, how to empathize, how to lead, follow and collaborate. These are the life skills no worksheet can teach.

As mentioned, by the time they left us for kindergarten, our kids knew their letters, numbers, and other academic milestones - yes. (As teachers, we love to brag about our students!) But they also knew how to speak up, how to listen, how to wait their turn, how to bounce back when things didn't go their way. They knew how to work as a team and how to navigate conflict with kindness. They had a toolbox of emotional intelligence that would carry them far.

And let's be honest—that's the stuff that really matters.

When parents would ask, "Are they ready for kindergarten?" I could smile with full confidence and say, "They're more than ready. Academically, socially, emotionally—they've got this."

Because while the world might measure success in grades and test scores, we knew the truth: children are born learners. Our job was simply to give them a place to grow, explore, and discover the joy of becoming exactly who they're meant to be.

And if they happened to do it with glue in their hair and stickers on their shoes—well, even better.

Chapter 7: Learning Through Play (The Real Work)

If you ask a preschooler what they did at school today, the answer is almost always the same: "Play" or, as they get older, "Nothing." (Cue the shoulder shrug as well.)

To the untrained eye, it might look like a room full of children gathered around in small centers, laughing, making messes, and seemingly doing everything but learning. But here's the secret—play is where the real magic happens.

While adults might think of learning as sitting still and listening, preschoolers learn by doing. They count while stacking blocks, experiment with physics while launching toy cars, and practice social skills by arguing over who gets to be the teacher in pretend school.

Despite the chaos, the mess, and the occasional glitter-related trauma, creative time was one of the most important parts of early childhood education. It taught kids confidence. It taught them problem-solving. It helped them express themselves in ways that words sometimes couldn't.

But beyond the paintbrushes and googly eyes, there was so much real learning happening—quietly, joyfully, and sometimes in disguise.

Our curriculum was thoughtfully built around the belief that kids learn best when they're engaged—not just instructed. We followed a robust academic foundation rooted in hands-on, play-based learning. Yes, we taught basic reading, writing, and math skills, but our teachers also taught how to ask questions, how to wonder out loud, how to try something new without being afraid of getting it wrong.

And here's where I'd like to go on a little tangent and wish more elementary schools incorporated centers, hands-on learning, open-ended curriculum, and other learning opportunities that weave real-life learning together with student interests and technology. Imagine the possibilities if we brought the best knowledge and opportunities to each student this way!

But back to the heart of it all: play is not a break from learning—it IS learning. And anyone who's ever spent time with a preschooler knows that they take their play very, very seriously.

***

Now, this brings me to the great "playing is learning" debate that every preschool teacher has had with a well-meaning but skeptical parent:

Parent: "But when do they actually learn?"

Me: "They're learning all day long!"

Parent: "…But when do they do, you know, real school stuff?"

This is always my cue to explain that playing *is* real school stuff. Every time a child builds a tower, tells a story, or experiments with mixing colors, they're learning essential skills.

I remember one particular conversation that perfectly illustrates this point. A mom asked me, "Why don't you do more worksheets?"

I smiled and pointed across the room to her daughter, who was kneeling in the dramatic play area, "writing" down food orders for the pretend restaurant. She had a notepad in one hand, a crayon in the other, and a very serious look on her face.

I asked her, "What are you doing?"

Without missing a beat, she said, "Writing a menu! And a shopping list. And a note for my chef so he remembers to make cookies."

The mom watched her daughter "scribbling" (pre-writing skills), asking questions (language development), and problem-solving how to keep the "kitchen" running smoothly (executive functioning).

I turned to the mom and said, "That's why."

She never asked about worksheets again.

***

Of course, not all play looks the same, and each type teaches something different. For example, a song sung in Spanish with a catchy tune will teach a child more than any stack of flashcards ever could. Let me walk you through some of the most powerful types of play I've witnessed.

First, there's what I like to call the "Preschool Oscars"—dramatic play.

If you ever need proof that kids are natural-born storytellers, step into a preschool's dramatic play area.

One week, our dress-up corner was transformed into a doctor's office. Kids diagnosed each other with wild conditions ("You have too many giggles!"), prescribed creative treatments ("Three jumps and a hug should fix it!"), and demonstrated excellent bedside manners ("Don't be scared. I'll hold your hand.").

The very next week, it morphed into a bustling grocery store. Kids grabbed baskets, calculated pretend prices, and one child, in a very serious voice, asked, "Do you have a rewards card?"

Through dramatic play, they're mastering language, cooperation, and problem-solving—all while having an absolute blast.

Then there's sensory play, which I often joke is the reason why my floor is always covered in rice and shaving cream.

There's something about touching, squishing, and mixing things that preschoolers absolutely love. Hence, the reason there exists a billion different recipes for slime!

Sensory bins became one of my favorite ways to sneak in learning. One week, I filled a bin with dry rice, measuring cups, and tiny animal figurines. I watched as kids scooped, poured, and ran their fingers through the grains.

One child lined up the animals and started sorting them: "These are all the farm animals. These ones live in the jungle."

Another measured the rice in cups, declaring, "This one holds more than that one!"—an early math discovery happening right before my eyes.

And then there was Ashton, who simply enjoyed burying his hands in the rice and giggling.

All equally valid ways to learn.

But some of the most magical learning happens outside in what I call the kingdom of dirt and discovery, where the best discoveries are just waiting to be made.

One spring morning, a group of kids found a worm. This tiny creature became the center of a preschool-wide investigation.

"Where does he live?" "What does he eat?" "Can I keep him as a pet?"

Before I knew it, we were knee-deep in an impromptu science lesson, complete with drawing "worm homes" and carefully setting him free in the garden.

And just like that, outdoor play transformed into a lesson in biology, empathy ("He needs to be with his family!"), and responsibility ("We have to be gentle!").

***

Now, some of the most valuable lessons actually come from conflict resolution, and playtime is where these teachable moments truly shine. It's where learning happens in disguise, especially during those classic preschool arguments.

Take the classic "I had it first!" debate. Two kids, one toy, and the age-old struggle of who gets it now.

My favorite solution? The Timer Trick.

Two kids, two minutes each. The sand timer gets flipped, and they both watch as the grains slip through. The moment the last grain falls, the next child gets their turn.

What are they really learning in this simple exchange?

- Patience
- Fairness
- Time management ("Two minutes feels long when I'm waiting!")

It's amazing how many life lessons can be wrapped up in a simple toy dispute.

* * *

Here's the thing about kids—they have incredible imaginations. And sometimes, playtime takes some truly unexpected turns that remind you why this job is never boring. These moments often get weird and hilarious in the best possible way.

One day, the block area transformed into a performance hall. A group of kids built an elaborate "stage" and declared that four of their classmates were now in a band. (The chosen band members didn't seem to have much say in the matter.)

One child played air guitar with impressive enthusiasm, while another drummed enthusiastically on a table. The third looked genuinely confused about his role, and the fourth sang a completely made-up song about butterflies that somehow became the hit of the day.

Another time, we had set up a library in our dramatic play area. A little girl walked up to me, handed me a book, and whispered sternly, "Shhh. No talking. Library rules."

She then proceeded to charge me pretend money for a late fee.

The entrepreneurial spirit was strong with that one.

***

At the end of the day, though, here's what I want you to take away from all of this: play is powerful. It isn't just something kids do—it's how they grow, learn, and make sense of the world around them.

Through play, they learn to work together, solve problems, explore new ideas, and express themselves. They practice empathy, independence, and confidence—all while having the time of their lives.

So when a child proudly tells me, "I played today!" I smile and say, "That's wonderful. Tell me all about it."

Because I know that in that play, they weren't just passing time.

They were learning.

They were working.

And they were becoming exactly who they were meant to be.

Chapter 8: The Teacher's Toolkit (And The Magic Within)

If you think preschool teachers just need crayons, construction paper, and a whiteboard to do their jobs, let me stop you right there. Sure, those are useful, but the real tools of the trade? They go way beyond school supplies.

A preschool teacher's toolkit isn't just about what's in the cabinets—it's about the secret skills, superpowers, and sheer magic they bring into the classroom every day. Because let's be honest: managing a room full of tiny humans is like conducting an orchestra while riding a rollercoaster—blindfolded.

So, what exactly is in a great preschool teacher's toolkit? Grab a juice box and settle in, because we're about to open the treasure chest.

Let's start with what I consider the most essential tool: the magic voice. Preschool teachers don't yell. Oh no. Yelling and raising your voice is rookie behavior. The real pros? They use "The Voice"—a careful balance of enthusiasm, authority, and just the right amount of *we are not negotiating, my dear child.* "The Voice" together with "The Look" is a superpower all teachers need to master!

For example, when a toddler is on the verge of an epic meltdown because their sock is feeling weird, a teacher doesn't panic. Instead, they lean in close, lower their voice, and say something like:

"Wow, that sock looks so interesting! I bet if we stretch it a little, it will feel just right! Want to try it together?"

Boom. Crisis averted. Tears dry up. Sock situation resolved.

Preschool teachers are basically hostage negotiators— but with more glitter and stickers.

Right alongside that magical voice sits what might be even more important: the infinite patience reserve. And let me tell you, it needs to be refilled daily—hopefully.

Patience isn't just a virtue in preschool—it's an absolute necessity.

Imagine this: You've just explained and demonstrated a simple craft project, and without fail, a child will raise their hand and ask, "What are we doing?"

You calmly repeat the instructions.

Another child stares at you, then asks, "Do we have to do this?"

You smile. Take a deep breath. You repeat the instructions again.

A third child: "I don't have a glue stick."

You look down. There is literally a glue stick in their hand.

It's in these moments that preschool teachers prove their superhuman ability to stay calm while resisting the urge to lie down in the middle of the playroom floor.

Of course, none of this would be possible without another essential tool: the ability to function on very little sleep and very much coffee.

Every preschool teacher I know is at least 50% caffeine and 50% magic. They wake up early, prepare lessons, manage classroom chaos, and still have the energy to genuinely care about each child's day.

Even on mornings when they spill their coffee, step on a rogue LEGO, and arrive at work only to realize they forgot to dress for the theme of the day—they show up with a smile.

But perhaps what sets great preschool teachers apart is their "I can handle anything" attitude.

Preschool teachers have a unique ability to deal with any and all crises without flinching. Let's take what I like to call The Morning from Hell as an example:

Our scheduled field trip venue just cancelled on us. Two parents lined up outside our offices to "talk" about changing their schedule during summer, while at the same time, a tour walks in and the phones are going crazy, and three teachers lined up asking, "Do you have a minute?"

Did the teachers panic? Nope. They handled it with the grace of Olympic athletes, juggling chaos like it was just another Tuesday.

Then there's what might be the most impressive superpower of all: knowing every child's needs instantly.

Within days of meeting their students, preschool teachers somehow know who needs extra hugs in the morning, who only eats food if it's cut into triangles, who is about to have a meltdown before even they realize it, which child will always forget their lunch, and which child will always have extra snacks (and will share if bribed correctly).

It's like they have a sixth sense for toddler emotions.

Closely related to this is their mastery of the art of distraction. Any experienced preschool teacher knows the best way to stop a potential meltdown is a well-placed distraction.

For example:

Child (on the verge of a meltdown): "I WANTED THE YELLOW CUP!"

Teacher (thinking fast): "Oh wow, did you see that bird outside? It looks like it's waving at you!"

Child (suddenly intrigued): "Where?"

And just like that, the tantrum is gone. Preschool teachers could probably broker world peace with their distraction skills.

Now, we can't forget about one of the most powerful tools in the arsenal: the ultimate "Mom Look" (even if they're not a mom).

Preschool teachers have a look—a single raised eyebrow that can stop a child from shoving Play-Doh up their nose or sneaking someone else's snack.

This look is so powerful, it could probably stop a speeding train. Essential to successful job performance if you are a teacher of any age.

But here's where the real artistry comes in: the ability to make everything sound fun, even clean-up time.

Getting preschoolers to clean up is like herding cats— unless you make it a game.

Teachers don't say, "Pick up the blocks."

They say, "Let's see who can pick up the most blocks in 30 seconds! Ready... GO!"

And suddenly, those same kids who didn't want to clean are now speed-running like Olympic champions.

Perhaps one of the most crucial tools, though, is the emotional resilience of a warrior.

Teaching preschool means dealing with a lot of emotions—tiny humans have big feelings.

Some days, kids run up to their teacher for hugs like they're long-lost family members. Other days, they cry over absolutely nothing (i.e., their banana broke in half, or they wanted to be first in line but also last in line at the same time).

And through it all, the teachers stay kind, patient, and understanding—because they know that to a four-year-old, even a broken banana is a very big deal.

But at the heart of every great preschool teacher's toolkit is something that can't be taught or learned from any manual: the endless love for the job, even on the hard days.

At the end of the day, preschool teachers don't do it for the paycheck (because let's be real, they should be paid triple).

They do it because they love the kids. Because they believe in early childhood education. Because they know they're shaping little lives in ways that will last forever.

They celebrate the small victories—like when a child finally writes their name correctly or shares their favorite toy without prompting. They cheer when a shy kid makes their first friend. They beam with pride when their students leave for kindergarten, knowing they helped prepare them for the next big step.

***

A preschool teacher's toolkit isn't just about glue sticks and lesson plans. It's about patience, creativity, a deep love for what they do, and sharing it with the world. The magic truly lives on in everything they do.

They may not wear capes (well, except on superhero day), but make no mistake—preschool teachers are real-life superheroes. And the magic they bring to the classroom? It's the kind that stays with kids forever.

There is always that one teacher (or a couple if you're lucky) that everyone seems to have in their lives. The one who listened, brought out the best in them, believed in them when even they didn't think they could. Preschool teachers truly embed themselves in the life of their children. Their love for the child goes beyond the classroom, and they become a part of dinner conversations with parents and the child at home. They are the family your child has when parents go off to work. And that responsibility is an incredible honor for all us Early Childhood Educators. To be trusted with your child is the most precious gift for us.

These were the moments that mattered. By the time they left us for kindergarten, our kids were academically prepared—but more importantly, they were brave, curious, kind, and full of wonder. That's the real work of early childhood. And if they remember and talk about their teachers years down the line, that's the ultimate bonus for us!

Chapter 9: Parent-Teacher Partnerships (And The Occasional Miscommunication)

O ne of the most fascinating things about running a preschool is that you're not just dealing with children—you're also working with their parents. And if you think tiny humans are unpredictable, just wait until you meet their grown-ups.

The relationship between parents and teachers is a delicate dance. When it works, it's beautiful—like a perfectly choreographed ballet. When it doesn't... well, let's just say it's more like a three-year-old's first attempt at interpretive dance.

At its core, a strong parent-teacher partnership is built on trust, communication, and a shared goal: helping children grow into happy, confident, capable little people. But getting there? That's where things get interesting.

***

Let me start with one of my favorite types of conversations: the "My child would never..." discussions.

Every preschool teacher has been in a meeting with a parent who, upon hearing that their little angel might have misbehaved, gasps in shock and says, "My child would never do that."

Oh, but they would. And they did.

For example:

Me: "So, today during snack time, Jack decided to test the laws of physics by painting applesauce all over himself."

Parent: "Oh, that's impossible. Jack doesn't even like applesauce."

Me (gesturing to the applesauce-stained clothes): "Well… he seemed pretty passionate about it today."

These conversations are always handled with care. No parent wants to hear that their child was the one who convinced the entire class that the bathroom soap dispenser was actually a volcano that needed erupting. But honesty is key, and the best parents are the ones who understand that even the sweetest kids have their moments.

On the flip side, there are the parents who are convinced that their child is a misunderstood prodigy, leading to what I call the "Is my child a genius?" discussions.

Parent: "Riley is very advanced for her age. I think she's ready for quantum physics."

Me: "Riley tried to eat a crayon today."

It's wonderful when parents are excited about their child's development, but sometimes expectations need a gentle reality check. Yes, little Riley might have an incredible vocabulary, but she also just tried to put her shoe in the toilet. Balance is important.

That being said, every child has their own unique strengths, and part of a teacher's job is to help parents recognize and celebrate those—whether it's an early love for storytelling, a knack for problem-solving, or a deep passion for digging holes in the playground.

Then there's what I've learned to call the "Can I just speak to you for a minute?" trap. Preschool teachers quickly learn that when a parent says this, it is never just a minute. It is at least 20 minutes—possibly longer if they've had coffee.

Sometimes, these conversations are lovely. A parent wants to share how much their child loves school, or they have a cute story about something their child said at home.

Other times, the conversation starts with, "So, I was on Google last night…" and that's when you know you're about to go down a rabbit hole of internet research, conspiracy theories about gluten, and a discussion on whether blue food coloring is really safe, all while other parents are trying to also drop off their kids and talk to you.

Tip to parents: Best to have these conversations during naptime, or by scheduling a time to meet.

***

Speaking of drop-off, let's talk about the art of drop-off and pick-up diplomacy.

Mornings at preschool are a carefully orchestrated event. The goal is simple: parents drop off their children, children say goodbye without turning it into a Broadway production, and parents leave.

However, it doesn't always go smoothly. Some children are clingy. Some parents are clingy. Some parents try to negotiate extended goodbyes as if they're dropping their child off at an airport for an international flight rather than for a three-hour preschool session.

Then, there are the stealth drop-offs—where a parent will literally disappear while their child is distracted, leading to a sudden, dramatic realization 30 seconds later:

"WAIT. WHERE'S MOMMY?!"

Cue tears, wails of betrayal, and the teacher trying to reassure the child that, no, Mommy has not abandoned them forever, and yes, she will definitely be back at pick-up time.

And somehow, even with all this careful orchestration, we still end up with the mystery of the missing items. Every preschool has a Lost and Found box overflowing with items that should have been reunited with their rightful owners long ago. But for some reason, certain parents never seem to recognize their own child's belongings.

Me: "This jacket has been in the lost and found for two months. Does it belong to your son?"

Parent: "No, I don't think so."

Me: "It has his name written inside it."

Parent: "Oh! Maybe it does, then."

And then there's the infamous "missing" shoe/lunchbox/backpack dilemma. Somehow, even in a controlled indoor environment, one child will always end up leaving with only one hair bow in their pigtails. Where did the other bow go? No one knows. It has vanished into the preschool void, alongside dozens of lost socks and tiny water bottles.

***

Now, let's dive into one of my absolute favorites: the "My child only eats…" challenge.

Every preschool teacher has encountered a parent who insists their child will only eat a highly specific menu of foods.

Parent: "Olivia will only eat organic, gluten-free, dairy-free, sugar-free, non-GMO, ethically sourced apples from a specific farm in Vermont."

Me: "Interesting. Because I just watched Olivia eat three chicken nuggets at our Friendship Party."

The truth is, kids eat what's available when they're hungry. They might refuse broccoli at home but devour it at school just because another kid is eating it. Peer pressure at the lunch table is real, and sometimes it works in everyone's favour.

This brings up something I see all the time: the spectrum of parental involvement. Some parents email. Some text. Some call. Some do all three—daily. Then, there are the parents who forget they even have a child enrolled in preschool until it's time to pick them up.

The best relationships are somewhere in between. Good parent-teacher partnerships are about open communication, trust, and respect. When parents and teachers work together, kids thrive.

***

But perhaps my favorite question of all is the one I get at least once a week, when a parent will stare at their child's teacher in wide-eyed amazement and say, "I don't know how you do this all day."

The answer? We love it.

Yes, it's exhausting. Sure, there are days when it feels like we're herding wild puppies in a room full of squeaky toys. But there's nothing quite like watching a child learn, grow, and discover the world.

At the end of the day, the best teachers and the best parents have one thing in common: they want what's best for the child. And when that partnership works, it's pure magic.

Because whether we're dealing with lost shoes, snack-time negotiations, or spontaneous tantrums over who gets to be first in line, we're all in this together—raising the next generation, one tiny, sticky hand at a time.

Chapter 10: The Teacher's Lounge

Every preschool has one—that sacred little spot that smells faintly of coffee, crayons, and exhaustion—the teacher's lounge. Ours was more than just a break room; it was the cozy, cluttered command center and the true heartbeat of the school.

It was a small space, which meant you were always bumping into a coworker, squeezing past a chair, or sharing a quick laugh (or vent) before running back into the chaos. On the surface, it looked like a normal office with a couple of computers, some barstools and chairs, and a commercial-grade printer that hummed along like it had its own mission in life. But anyone who stepped inside knew this wasn't just a room. It was where real stories were shared, sanity was restored, and sometimes, brilliant ideas for things like Summer Camp themes were born in the middle of a five-minute coffee break.

At the start of the week, the lounge always looked neat and tidy. But by Friday afternoon? Different story. Counters were covered with an organized chaos of "pre-loved" toys, books, crayons, markers, and extra supplies teachers had left behind for others to use. Because let's be honest, the greatest sin in preschool is throwing anything away.

It was a sacred space for adult conversations, a quiet moment to breathe, and a place our Directors worked hard to make feel like home. They'd leave out announcements, snacks, or little notes of encouragement to lift spirits. In its own way, that tiny, cluttered lounge was a confessional, a therapy office, a planning hub, and occasionally, the set of a sitcom no one could ever script.

***

Let's start with the one universal truth in early childhood education: teachers run on coffee and snacks. It's not a preference, it's a survival mechanism. This brings me to what I call the great coffee crisis.

Unfortunately, coffee in a preschool setting is a risky endeavour. You make a cup, get called to handle a potty accident, and return to find your coffee ice-cold. Reheat it, get summoned to break up an intense debate over whose turn it is on the playground, return, and find your coffee missing entirely.

It's a vicious cycle.

The worst days? When the coffee machine breaks.

I remember one tragic morning when we discovered the Keurig had cracked. There was an audible silence, followed by a slow, dramatic sigh from the lead teacher. Someone whispered, "We're not going to make it."

An emergency Starbucks run was authorized. Priorities, people.

Speaking of sustenance, this leads me to what I've dubbed the "lunch roulette" experience. A teacher's lunch break is a mythical event that exists in theory but rarely in reality. If you're lucky, you get five minutes to eat something that doesn't require refrigeration, utensils, or chewing.

But the true test of a teacher's stomach is Lunch Roulette—where you attempt to eat while ignoring the scent of glue, Play-Doh, and whatever unidentifiable mystery odor is floating through the hallway, or from your article of clothing.

One of my colleagues once bit into a sandwich only to hear, "Ms. Jen, Brayden just licked the glue stick."

She put the sandwich down. Lunch was over. And that was it.

Lunch is treasured time to be an adult. And scrumptious adult food that doesn't appear on the kids' menu is priceless. This is why food is one of our top love languages at preschools.

**

Now, the teacher's lounge also serves as the setting for what I like to call group therapy sessions, though we officially call them team meetings.

Teacher's lounge conversations usually begin with someone dramatically collapsing onto a chair and declaring, *"You won't believe what just happened."* Everyone listens. Everyone nods. Everyone understands.

Some classic teacher lounge moments include the tale of the missing lunch box (how do kids lose their lunch box in a completely enclosed classroom?), the toddler rebellion (when every child simultaneously decides *"No"* is the only word they will acknowledge), the accidental permanent marker incident (self-explanatory, and always unfortunate), and the Mysterious Wet Spot (best not to investigate further). These venting sessions are crucial. Without them, we'd all be rocking in the corner whispering the alphabet song to ourselves.

And then, there's what we've come to know as the "parent email breakdown." There's a very specific sigh reserved for opening an email from *that* parent—the one who writes six-paragraph essays about why their child should get more circle time and less snack time. Once, we even had a parent send us a full PowerPoint presentation on why their son should not be required to participate in finger painting. Another emailed a photo of a microscopic scratch on their daughter's knee, demanding to know the "exact series of events that led to this tragedy."

Cue the teacher lounge debrief:

"It's just a tiny scratch."

"Did they want a formal investigation?"

"I think we need CSI: Preschool Edition."

But the lounge wasn't only for comedy. It was also where we leaned on each other during the hardest moments, the ones that made you want to curl up and cry into your coffee cup.

I remember late one afternoon, Ms. Taylor, one of our newer teachers, was hunched over her phone in the lounge, staring at a list of numbers with pure dread written across her face. Ms. Grace and Ms. Alicia walked in, caught sight of her expression, and instantly knew that look.

"Rough one?" Grace asked gently.

Ms. Taylor sighed, her voice barely above a whisper. "I have to call Julian's parents and tell them he bit Luca. And then I have to call Luca's parents. I feel like I'm walking a tightrope."

Without hesitation, Alicia walked over and put a hand on her shoulder. "Take a deep breath. We've all been there. You're part of the team, and you're not alone in this."

They pulled up chairs, turning the moment into an impromptu coaching session. First came the detective work: what exactly happened before the bite? Was it during a transition? Was Julian frustrated over a toy? Then, the plan: shadow him the next day, give him a little space from Luca, and watch for patterns that might explain his biting triggers.

Ms. Taylor scribbled notes and then asked, almost timidly, "But what do I say to the parents?"

"With Julian's parents," Alicia explained, "you're a partner. Tell them the facts, ask if anything has changed at home, and share the plan we've made. They'll get an incident report at pick-up, and we'll schedule a conference soon."

"With Luca's parents," Grace added, "you're the professional. Reassure them he's safe, explain what happened without naming names, and walk them through what we're doing to prevent it from happening again. They need to hear that their child's safety is our first priority."

By the end, Ms. Taylor's shoulders had relaxed. She looked up, managing a small, grateful smile. "Thank you. I think I can do this now."

"Of course you can," Alicia told her with a grin. "And tomorrow, we'll solve the mystery of the biter."

That was the lounge at its best: equal parts comedy club, therapy office, and crisis center. A place for sighs, laughter, comfort, and solidarity. This was where the real stories happened.

***

Then there are the days that test every ounce of training and patience we have—what I call the substitute teacher chronicles, featuring our "floater" teachers.

Bringing in a substitute teacher is like throwing a wrench into a finely tuned machine. No matter how detailed the lesson plan, the day is going to be… interesting.

One floater, bless her heart, didn't realize toddlers are opportunists. She turned her back for five seconds—just enough time for three kids to take off their jackets right before going outside, one to hide under the table, and another to start a "parade" that led half the class out the door.

The teacher's lounge consensus? She tried her best.

And then there are those juggling-everything-at-once days when life decides to test your limits all at the same time. Let's set the scene: the fire alarm went off by accident at the exact moment our new students, McKenzie and Mason, walked in for their very first day. The snacks were running late, two teachers needed a potty break, and somehow, we were expected to keep it all together with sheer willpower and dry shampoo.

As if that wasn't enough, the enrollment paperwork had prepared us for one new child named *McKenzie Mason.* We made cubbie tags, name labels, everything. So when the doors opened and in walked not just McKenzie Mason but McKenzie *and* Mason, we realized we'd been prepping for one kid… and got twins. Cue the death stare straight at poor Ms. Ellianne, our enrollment director, who later admitted she'd enrolled the family without the kids even present. The teachers' reactions were priceless—equal parts shock, laughter, and "are you kidding me right now?" It was absolute chaos, but honestly, that's what makes this work so memorable. And what do teachers do in these moments? We laugh. We smile. Because if we don't, we'd stress—and surviving these curveballs is kind of our superpower.

***

But perhaps what bonds teachers together most is what I call the "inside jokes that make no sense" club.

Spending your days in a room full of preschoolers does something to your brain. Over time, certain phrases and moments become legendary.

Some classic teacher lounge catchphrases include:

- "Do you need to go potty?" (said to a fully grown adult, out of habit)
- "Why is there a puzzle piece in the toilet?"
- "We do not lick the floor, remember?"
- "How did you get glue in your hair again?"
- "No, pants are not optional."

If an outsider overheard our conversations, they'd assume we were completely unhinged. And maybe we are.

***

At the end of each day comes the reality check moment. After the last child has been picked up, there's always a moment where teachers just sit.

The glitter has settled. The last juice box has been spilled. The classroom looks like a tornado hit it. Someone finds a lone sock and wonders, "Who did this belong to?"

And in the teacher's lounge, we exhale. We swap stories, we celebrate the small victories, and we remind each other why we do this.

Because despite the chaos, despite the messes, despite the four surprise fire drills in one week—this job is filled with magic.

We get to watch children grow, learn, and become little people who will one day take on the world. And that? That makes every spilled coffee, lost shoe, and mysterious wet spot completely worth it.

So tomorrow, we'll do it all over again. But first, let's fix that coffee machine.

Chapter 11: The Heart of It All

They don't tell you, when you open a preschool, that you're also signing up to be a therapist, event planner, crisis manager, mentor, grief counselor, and cheerleader—sometimes all in the same day. I used to think I was building a school. It took years to realize I was actually building a family.

As the years went by and our little preschool turned into a multi-campus community, I found myself stepping into a new kind of role. I wasn't the one wiping noses or leading circle time anymore. I had moved from teacher to leader, and with that shift came a deeper understanding of what it meant to be the one who sets the tone.

The classrooms were no longer just filled with children learning—they were filled with teachers growing. And I knew my job had become something else entirely: to care for the people who cared for the children.

When people talk about leadership, they often speak in corporate terms—vision statements, management styles, productivity. But in early childhood, leadership looks a lot more like handwritten notes, last-minute grocery runs for birthday cupcakes, and keeping it together when your teachers are falling apart. The weight and the wonder of it all hit me differently than I expected.

There was the teacher who quietly told me she was going through a divorce and didn't want anyone to know. So we adjusted her schedule, supported her behind the scenes, and gave her space to grieve in her own time.

There was the assistant teacher who called me in tears after her car broke down—not because she needed help with the car, but because she didn't want to let her class down. So we picked her up. We made it work.

And there were so many days when I sat in my office at 6 p.m., lights off, just breathing. Because the emotional load of running a preschool is heavy. Joyful, but heavy. When you are taking people's money and their children, the two things that are most valuable to parents, it's not "just business." Everything is "personal." You care. You love. Your heart is invested in the children and their families. You protect. You go home thinking about the students. You carry this joy and the responsibility of the job knowing it's a gift. You are someone's lifeline. Their hero. A part of their family. Loved.

***

I came to realize that success in early childhood isn't measured in enrollment numbers or inspection scores. It's measured in teacher retention, parent hugs at pick-up, and the way a teacher's eyes light up when they're seen—really seen—by their leadership. This became my philosophy of putting people first.

I always said, "We read with our hearts before we teach with our minds." That wasn't just a motto—it was the foundation of our culture.

We celebrated birthdays and weddings, new babies and new beginnings. We created a space where it was okay to say, "I'm not okay today." And somehow, that honesty made us stronger.

***

Then came the day that changed everything: the pandemic.

Like everyone else in education, we were thrown into chaos overnight. There was fear, confusion, and an overwhelming sense of responsibility. I remember walking into an empty classroom during lockdown—toys untouched, chairs stacked, silence echoing where laughter used to be. It broke me.

But it also clarified everything. We pivoted, adapted, sanitized until our hands cracked, and showed up however we could. Zoom circle time. Drive-by parking lot graduations. Emergency care for essential workers only. And layered on top of all that? The confusing COVID procedures. Fifteen-day quarantines for a single sniffle. Endless reporting to health departments. Mask mandates for two-year-olds—as if a toddler is going to keep one on longer than five seconds. And let's not forget the six-foot distancing rule legislators somehow thought preschoolers could follow. (If you've ever seen toddlers in a classroom, you know they're basically magnets in motion.) Through it all, our team didn't just survive—they showed up like superheroes, day after day.

And through it all, the love stayed. The mission didn't change.

What stands out most from that time wasn't just the logistics or the constant rule changes—it was the way our team came together. We checked in on each other daily, swapped encouragement and funny stories in our brand-new WhatsApp group, and made silly videos just to keep spirits up. More than anything, we just missed the noise of our school—the hustle, the bustle, the chatter of kids and teachers that made every day feel alive.

Our families showed up for us too. Parents sent heartwarming messages, checking in on us when we were the ones usually checking in on them. (Okay, mixed in were a couple of desperate "When will you open? I have to work!" texts, but even those came from a place of survival we all understood.) In a strange way, the human connection during that time felt stronger than ever. It was raw, it was honest, and it reminded us that preschool was never just a service—it was a community.

***

While leading my schools, I was also raising my boys—Preston, Pierce, and Parker. There were seasons when I felt like I was giving my best self to the school and only what was left over to my family. The guilt sat on my chest like a stone. This became my ongoing challenge of balancing two worlds: mom and owner.

It's true. The struggle to balance being a mom and a business owner was a constant, and at times, a comical battle. For a long time, the guilt felt crushing—a heavy weight that followed me everywhere. The universe, in its infinite wisdom, decided to send me a wake-up call in the form of my son.

I remember one afternoon, rushing through Target to grab a few things. Parker, my youngest, was riding in the cart when I tossed in a pack of stickers. He looked at me, his little brow furrowed, and asked the question that absolutely killed me: *"Are those for me, or for your other kids?"* My own three-year-old saw himself as just another one of the many children I was responsible for, held to the same standard as 150+ preschool kids. That moment, as heartbreaking as it was, became a pivot point. It was a hilarious, terrible, beautiful realization that I was living in two worlds and that the line between them was blurrier than I thought.

I didn't know any other way than to lead with my heart. At home, I was mom. At school, I treated every child with the same love, respect, and kindness as I gave my own boys—and no less.

I remember taking a call during one of Preston's baseball games—sneaking away from the bleachers to talk to a frantic teacher. I handled it, returned to my seat, and tried to be present. But the truth was, I lived in two worlds—and I was always torn between them.

And then there was Pierce. My beautiful son with special needs, who reminded me daily that patience, grace, and unconditional love are more powerful than any curriculum. He grounded me. He reminded me what this was all about. But even with that deep-seated purpose, the guilt still crept in. There were countless times I felt terrible for not being able to take him to every single therapy session.

And just like in *My Big Fat Greek Wedding*, my big, beautiful family always stepped in. My parents, my siblings, my in-laws—they were my village. They made sure my boys never felt less than. Somehow, Pierce made it to every therapy session, Preston made it to basketball or baseball practice, and Parker made it to school every day with mommy.

Looking back, the desire to be more present for my own boys, to not miss a single school pickup or drop-off, became my greatest motivation. It drove me to hire the most talented, qualified, and loving people I could find for my schools. It wasn't always easy to let go, but when the time came, I had no problem delegating. I trusted my incredible management teams to handle things so I could be where I needed to be—with my family. And looking back, I'm so glad I did.

***

For every glitter-covered emergency or licensing panic, there were moments that made everything worth it—the moments that truly matter.

Like the little boy who started the year nonverbal—and left singing the ABCs to his baby sister. Or the mom who cried at graduation, whispering, "I was terrified to leave my child with anyone… and now I wish they could stay here forever."

Those moments don't come with awards. But they stay with you.

Eventually, it came time to sell my schools—a decision made with equal parts sadness and peace. I knew my family needed me in a different way. And I knew I had left my schools better than I found them. Learning to let go so something could grow was one of the hardest lessons I had to learn.

Walking away was hard. But what I carry with me is this:

We didn't just run schools. We built legacies. We gave children their first safe space outside home. We gave teachers their calling. We gave families a village.

And at the center of it all was love.

Leadership in early childhood is not about having the right answers. It's about asking the right questions. It's not about policies—it's about people. It's not about perfection—it's about presence.

So to every owner, director, teacher, and parent who's doing the work: I see you. I've been you. And I believe in what you're building.

Because if you lead with love, you can't go wrong.

Chapter 12: Lessons Learned

Running a preschool for over a decade wasn't just about teaching kids—it was about learning from them. And trust me, kids are some of the best teachers out there. They don't hold back. They speak the truth (sometimes brutally). They live in the moment. And if you're paying attention, they teach you lessons that no business book or leadership seminar ever could.

This chapter is about the lessons I learned—not just from the experience of running a preschool, but from the tiny humans who filled its classrooms with laughter, tears, and more than a little chaos.

The first and perhaps most important lesson was the art of adaptability. Nothing ever goes exactly as planned—and that's okay.

I'm a planner by nature. I live by my color-coded calendar, to-do lists, and having a solid plan for the day. But preschoolers? They don't care about your plans.

There were days when I walked into the building with a neatly laid-out schedule, only to have it completely derailed before 9:00 AM. Maybe a kid had a meltdown because their favorite stuffed animal was left at home. Maybe three teachers called in sick at once. Maybe the class mascot stuffed turtle (Tiny Tim) had somehow escaped its cage and was now hiding somewhere in the art supply closet.

The best preschool teachers (and leaders) aren't the ones who stick rigidly to their plans. They're the ones who know how to pivot.

I quickly learned that flexibility was my superpower. If something wasn't working, we found a new way. If a lesson plan bombed, we tried something else. And if the kids decided that today was the day they were all dinosaurs, well… we just had a dinosaur-themed day.

In life and in business, the ability to adapt is priceless.

Related to this flexibility was another crucial lesson: patience is a muscle that needs constant strengthening. You think you're patient? Spend five minutes trying to get a room full of toddlers to put on their shoes.

Patience is not something you're born with—it's something you build over time.

At first, I thought I was patient. I mean, how hard could it be to work with small children? The answer: very.

Have you ever tried reasoning with a three-year-old about why they can't eat Play-Doh? Have you ever waited 15 minutes for a child to finish a sentence because they keep getting distracted mid-thought? Have you ever had to explain, again, why we don't put our fingers in our noses and then immediately touch our friends?

These moments tested my patience like nothing else. But over time, I realized something: patience isn't just about staying calm—it's about truly listening, understanding, and responding with empathy.

And let's be honest, most adults could use a little more patience in their daily lives, too.

***

One of the most beautiful things about working with kids is that they see magic in the tiniest things.

A child finally learns to zip up their coat? Victory dance time!

Cue the applause! Someone remembers to say "please" without being reminded!

And my personal favorite? A formerly shy kid speaks up for the first time. Best moment ever!

In the world of adults, we often wait for the "big wins" before we celebrate. We don't acknowledge progress until we hit a major milestone. But kids? They find joy in the process.

Watching their enthusiasm made me realize how much I was missing out on. I started celebrating the small wins in my own life, and it made all the difference.

When you start recognizing every little success, life feels a lot more joyful.

Working with so many different children also taught me that there's no one-size-fits-all approach. Every child is different—and so is every person.

One of the biggest mistakes I made early on was thinking that what worked for one child would work for all. Spoiler: it didn't.

Some kids needed structure. Others thrived in free play. Some kids loved group activities. Others needed quiet time. Some needed extra reassurance. Others wanted independence.

Once I realized that there's no single "right" way to teach, lead, or parent, everything changed.

This applies to adults, too. Not everyone learns the same way. Not everyone thrives in the same environment. The best leaders, teachers, and managers recognize this—and adjust their approach accordingly.

***

Another powerful lesson came from watching how children handle setbacks: mistakes are just part of the process.

Kids fall down a lot. But here's the thing: they don't dwell on it. They might cry for a moment, but then they get back up and try again.

Adults? We're terrible at this.

We're so afraid of failing that sometimes we don't even try. We overanalyze, overthink, and beat ourselves up when things don't go perfectly. But kids? They just keep going.

Watching preschoolers struggle, stumble, and get back up—over and over—was one of the greatest lessons I ever learned. Failure isn't the opposite of success. It's part of it.

But the most important lesson of all was this: love and kindness matter more than anything. At the end of the day, people just want to feel safe, loved, and valued.

Kids don't care how much you know until they know how much you care.

It didn't matter how perfect my lesson plans were or how organized my classroom was—if a child didn't feel loved, supported, and safe, nothing else mattered.

And honestly? The same applies to adults.

We all want to feel valued. We all want to be treated with kindness. We all thrive when we're surrounded by people who believe in us.

The best teachers, leaders, and humans are the ones who lead with love.

***

Finally, the hardest lesson I learned was that you can't pour from an empty cup. Taking care of yourself isn't selfish—it's necessary.

Preschool teachers give everything to their students. But here's the problem: burnout is real.

There were days when my teachers gave so much of themselves to the school that they had nothing left for their own families, myself included.

I learned (the hard way) that self-care isn't just a luxury—it's a necessity. If you don't take care of yourself, you can't take care of anyone else.

Whether you're a teacher, a parent, or a business owner, you have to set boundaries, prioritize rest, and give yourself grace.

Chapter 13: The Future of Early Childhood

The world of early childhood education is constantly evolving. New research, technologies, and societal changes influence how we teach, care for, and nurture young children. While some things remain timeless—like the magic of storytime or the joy of finger painting—other aspects of early education must adapt to meet the needs of modern families.

But here's the thing: the future of early childhood education isn't just in the hands of policymakers or educators—it's in the hands of every parent, caregiver, and advocate who believes in the power of a strong foundation for children.

When I first started my preschool, the biggest debates were around curriculum choices—Montessori vs. play-based vs. academic-focused programs. These conversations still exist, but today, early childhood education faces even bigger challenges and opportunities in our changing landscape.

The role of technology presents both promise and concern. Screens are everywhere, and while technology has incredible educational potential, it also raises concerns about attention spans, social skills, and physical activity. How do we balance screen time with real-world play and interaction? And how will AI effect the role of teachers?

There's also a growing recognition of the importance of mental health and emotional well-being. More than ever, we understand that teaching children how to manage emotions, build resilience, and develop empathy is just as critical as teaching them their ABCs.

Meanwhile, we're facing serious teacher shortages and burnout. The pandemic and other societal shifts have led to a growing teacher shortage in early childhood education. Low pay, high stress, and increasing expectations have made it harder to retain passionate educators.

And accessibility and affordability remain major hurdles. High-quality early childhood education is still out of reach for many families. The cost of care is rising, and in many 'good' schools, there are long waitlists and limited availability for parents trying to secure a spot for their child.

These are big issues, but the good news is that there are solutions—and we can all play a role in shaping them.

***

If we want high-quality early childhood education, we need to start by investing in our teachers—the people who make it all happen. Too often, early educators are underpaid and undervalued, despite playing one of the most critical roles in a child's development.

Here's what we can do: advocate for higher wages and better benefits for preschool teachers, provide professional development opportunities that keep educators engaged and growing, and create work environments that support teachers' mental and emotional well-being.

When teachers feel supported, they bring their best selves to the classroom—and that benefits everyone.

We also need to focus on bringing back the joy of learning. One of the things I loved most about my schools was the pure love and joy of learning. Kids were excited to come in, eager to explore, and fully engaged in their play. But as education systems push for more structured academics at younger ages, we risk losing that spark.

The future of early childhood education should embrace play-based learning that allows children to explore and discover at their own pace, outdoor education that connects kids with nature and encourages movement, making fitness and movement (whether as dance, games, sports programs, gym-play, etc.) an essential part of the curriculum, creative problem-solving activities that build critical thinking skills, and if possible, incorporating a second language (Sign Language, Spanish, etc.) into daily lesson plans. Kids are sponges, and can learn everything!

The goal isn't to rush kids into academics—it's to create an environment where they develop a love for learning that lasts a lifetime.

***

The truth is: sometimes what teachers really need isn't complicated at all. It's a heartfelt "thank you." It's a parent showing up to a conference, reading the newsletter we carefully put together, or just asking, "What do you need?" It's remembering that teachers are human too, with families, bills, struggles, and dreams of their own. A little grace and kindness go a long way.

Because here's the hard part, sometimes teachers feel invisible. Parents rush through drop-off like they're handing off a package, or assume "anyone can do this job." But not everyone can. And those moments of invisibility are heavy, which is why the little moments of recognition matter so much.

The magic that keeps us going isn't in mugs or scented candles. It's in the child with separation anxiety who finally runs into class smiling. It's in the nonverbal child who says their first word. It's in the former student who comes back years later and says, "You were my favorite teacher." It's in the parent who pauses long enough to say, "You made a difference in my child's life."

Those moments are worth more than anything else.

So if you want to shape the future of early childhood education, start here: support the people in the classrooms. Celebrate teachers. Remind them they are seen, valued, and deeply appreciated. Because when we invest in teachers, we invest in children. And when we invest in children, we invest in the future.

And if there's one thing I've learned from my years in the preschool world, it's this: children will always surprise us. They are resilient, curious, and full of potential. It's up to us to create a world where they—and their teachers—can thrive.

Because when we invest in early childhood education, we're not just shaping classrooms. We're shaping the future.

Chapter 14: Saying Goodbye

S aying goodbye is never easy. Whether it's a child moving on to kindergarten, a beloved teacher transitioning to a new chapter in their career, or, in my case, letting go of an entire preschool that had become my life's work—goodbyes in early childhood education come with a unique blend of heartbreak and hope.

For 15 years, my schools weren't just businesses; they were communities in which I lived and raised my family. They were places where parents trusted us with their most precious treasures, where teachers poured their hearts into nurturing young minds, and where thousands of little feet ran through the halls, leaving behind laughter, tears, and sticky fingerprints. When the time came for me to sell my schools, I knew it was the right decision—but that didn't make it any less emotional.

Every preschool owner and teacher gets used to the annual cycle of goodbyes during graduation—those first goodbyes when students move on. One minute, a shy three-year-old is clinging to their parent's leg on the first day of school, and before you know it, they're marching out the door in a tiny cap and gown, off to conquer kindergarten.

Graduation day at my schools was always bittersweet. The teachers and I would sit in the back, holding back tears as we watched our little ones proudly recite their ABCs and sing their goodbye songs. Parents snapped a thousand pictures, some of them getting teary-eyed themselves.

There were always a few kids who had been particularly attached to us—ones who ran to hug their teachers every morning, who insisted on sitting next to the same friend at snack time, who would hold my hand in the hallway just because. Watching them leave was like watching a piece of our hearts walk away.

But then, every once in a while, we'd get a surprise visit. A former student—now a towering middle schooler—would stop by with their parents to say hello.

"Do you remember me, Ms. Ashli?" they'd ask, grinning.

And even though they'd outgrown their baby faces and their tiny backpacks, I always did.

***

But the toughest goodbye was letting go of my schools entirely.

When I first opened my preschool, I never imagined the day I would walk away. It wasn't just a job; it was my identity. I had poured my heart, my soul, and countless sleepless nights into building something special.

But life has a way of nudging us toward new paths, even when we're not quite ready to take them. My son, Pierce, needed me more. My family needed me more. And deep down, I knew it was time.

The process of selling my schools was grueling—not just the legal and financial side of it, but the emotional weight of it all. How do you say goodbye to something you built from the ground up? How do you entrust your legacy to someone else and hope they carry it forward with the same love and dedication?

Handing over the keys felt surreal. I walked through the empty classrooms one last time, running my fingers along the tiny chairs and the art-covered walls. I thought about all the memories—the first steps taken, the first words spoken, the friendships formed. I thought about the teachers who had given so much of themselves to these children.

And then, I locked the doors behind me.

***

What no one tells you about letting go is that grief doesn't always hit you all at once. The unexpected grief comes in waves.

Some days, I was relieved—finally, a break from the never-ending to-do lists, the licensing inspections, the teaming challenges.

Other days, I felt lost. Who was I without my schools? Where did I belong if not in the world of early childhood education?

I missed the sound of children's laughter echoing through the hallways. I missed the tiny handprints on my office door and the hugs of each child. I missed seeing the teachers every day that I considered family. I missed being part of something bigger than myself.

There were moments when I questioned if I had made the right decision. Maybe I could have held on a little longer. Maybe I should have found a way to make it work.

But then, I'd remind myself of why I had let go. Because sometimes, saying goodbye isn't about giving up—it's about making space for something new.

***

In the weeks after selling my schools, I found myself drawn back to the world of early childhood education—but in a different way, and I discovered I was finding a new purpose. Instead of running preschools, I started mentoring other preschool owners. I helped them navigate the same challenges I had faced, offering advice, encouragement, and a listening ear.

I realized that even though I had said goodbye to my schools, I hadn't said goodbye to my passion. My love for early childhood education hadn't disappeared—it had simply evolved.

And then, something amazing happened. I started getting messages from former students' parents.

"Ms. Ashli, I just wanted to thank you. My daughter still talks about her time at your school. You made such a difference in her life."

"My son is thriving in kindergarten, and I know it's because of the foundation he got at your school."

"Just wanted you to know that your school was the best decision we ever made for our child."

"We just heard you sold your school. We are devastated!"

Every message was a reminder that my work hadn't ended when I sold my schools. The impact of what I had built would live on in every child who had walked through my doors.

***

Through this journey, I learned some powerful lessons about letting go. Change is scary, but it's also necessary—holding on too tightly to something, even something we love, can keep us from growing. The impact we make doesn't disappear—just because I no longer owned my schools didn't mean my work was erased. The children I had nurtured would carry those lessons with them forever. New beginnings come in unexpected ways—letting go of my schools didn't mean letting go of my purpose, it just meant finding new ways to pursue it. And it's okay to grieve—moving on doesn't mean we forget, and it's okay to miss what we left behind. It just means it mattered.

Now, when I think back on my time as a preschool owner, I don't just remember the challenges—the licensing battles, the endless paperwork, the teaming struggles. I remember the joy. The laughter. The moments of magic that made it all worth it.

And I know that while one chapter has ended, my story isn't over.

Because the thing about early childhood education—the thing that kept me going for all those years—is that it's never really about us. It's about the children. It's about the teachers who dedicate their lives to them. It's about the parents who trust us to care for their little ones.

And that? That never changes.

So here's to new beginnings. Here's to the teachers, the parents, the children who make this work so meaningful.

And here's to the magic that lives on—even after goodbye.

Chapter 15: The Magic Lives On

If there's one thing I've learned from my years as a preschool owner, it's that the magic of early childhood never really disappears. It doesn't fade when a child moves on to kindergarten. It doesn't vanish when a teacher retires. And even when a school changes ownership, the spirit of what was built remains, carried forward in the laughter, lessons, and love that once filled its walls.

Selling my schools was one of the hardest decisions I've ever made. But in the time since, I've come to realize that my impact didn't end when I handed over the keys. The magic—the heart of what I had built—was still alive in the children, the teachers, and the stories that came from those years of joyful chaos.

The thing about working in early childhood is that you don't always get to see the long-term effects of what you do. You help a child learn to share, tie their shoes, write their name, and then—poof—they're off to kindergarten, middle school, high school. You don't always know how the seeds you planted will grow. But every once in a while, you get a glimpse.

A few months after selling my schools, I received a message from a former parent: "Ms. Ashli, I don't know if you remember my son, Sterling, but I just wanted to tell you—he was named student of the month at his middle school! He still talks about his time at your preschool and how much he loved learning there. Thank you for giving him such a great start!"

Another day, I ran into a teenager at the grocery store. She was tall, confident, and had braces that reminded me she wasn't quite an adult yet.

"Ms. Ashli?" she asked, hesitantly.

I blinked, trying to place her. Then she smiled, and it clicked. "Samantha?"

She nodded. "You were my preschool teacher! I still remember the butterfly project we did. I loved that school so much."

We chatted for a few minutes, and as she walked away, I found myself smiling. Years had passed, but somehow, those tiny moments—the projects, the songs, the lessons—had stayed with her. That's when I realized: the magic of early childhood education isn't just about the time spent within the four walls of a classroom. It's about the foundation we build, the love we pour into these children, and the lessons they carry with them for a lifetime.

***

If the children are the heart of early childhood education, the teachers are its soul. Preschool teachers are superheroes in disguise, navigating tantrums, lost shoes, snack time debates, and spontaneous dance parties with the patience of saints and the energy of marathon runners. The best teachers understand that education isn't just about letters and numbers—it's about creating a safe, loving space where children feel seen, heard, and valued.

When I think back, I don't just think about the kids— I think about the incredible teachers who made the magic happen every single day. Ms. Maria could transform anything into a science lesson and was an exceptional "insectologist." Ms. Angie turned any lesson into a song, calming even the wildest toddler with her gentle voice. Mr. Forrest encouraged curiosity with his constant invitation to ask "why." Mrs. Margarita had the magic touch with infants, soothing them in seconds, while Ms. Cali knew how to turn even the roughest morning into a day of laughter. And let's not forget the directors—those organizational wizards who coordinated, supported, and juggled responsibilities with grace, keeping everything running while making it look effortless. Teachers like them are the kind of legacy that never fades.

***

Of course, there were always the stories—the endless stream of heartwarming, hilarious, and sometimes head-scratching moments that only happen in preschool. Like the time three-year-old Henry announced he was moving to the moon and packed a "suitcase" of Goldfish crackers and a stuffed animal. Or Isabella, who stood up mid-circle time to declare she had something *really important* to tell her mom, as though preschool were just a minor pit stop in her busy life. Or the infamous "pebble incident," when four children stuffed their pockets with tiny rocks, only to dissolve into tears when their parents later emptied them into the washing machine.

As silly as they may seem, these stories are proof of the wonder and joy that define early childhood—moments of discovery, curiosity, and pure, unfiltered magic. And the best part? The stories never stop.

As much as I love reminiscing, I also think a lot about the future. What will early childhood education look like in the years to come? How can we continue to nurture this magic in a world that is constantly changing? I worry sometimes—about the pressures placed on young children, about the increasing role of technology, about the decreasing respect for play as a fundamental part of learning.

But then I remember the teachers. The parents. The children themselves. I remember that as long as there are people who believe in the power of childhood—who fight for the importance of play, curiosity, and kindness—the magic will never truly fade. Maybe one day, one of my former students will open their own preschool. Maybe another will grow up to be a teacher, scientist, or artist, carrying the lessons of their earliest years with them. Maybe, in a decade or two, I'll walk past a playground and hear a child singing a song I used to teach.

Because the thing about early childhood education is that it doesn't just stay in one place—it ripples outward, shaping lives in ways we may never fully see.

***

So, as I close this chapter of my life, I do so with a heart full of gratitude. Gratitude for the children who taught me as much as I taught them. Gratitude for the teachers and directors who inspired me daily. Gratitude for the parents who trusted me with their most precious gifts.

The magic of childhood—the wonder, the laughter, the tiny triumphs and big emotions—will always be part of me. And while I may no longer run a preschool, I know this: the magic lives on. In every child and family who was ever part of my school. In every teacher who still sings silly songs and wipes away tears. In every story that makes us laugh, cry, and remember why we do what we do.

The magic of early childhood isn't something you can hold onto forever. But if you're lucky, you get to be part of it. And that is more than enough.

My Final Words

As you finish these pages, I want to thank you for walking this journey with me. Every story I shared was a piece of my heart, a memory of laughter, love, and even the chaos that made my years in early childhood so meaningful.

If you take only one thing away, I hope it is this: the magic of childhood is real. It lives in the sparkle of curiosity, in the warmth of a teacher's hug, and in the simple joy of watching a child discover something for the very first time. That magic doesn't belong just to schools or classrooms. It belongs to all of us who care for, guide, and love children.

Though my days of running preschools have ended, the lessons, the stories, and the joy continue to live in me, and I hope they now live a little in you too. May you always notice the small wonders, hold onto the laughter, and never forget that in every child's smile, the magic lives on.

With love and gratitude,

Ashli

www.ingramcontent.com/pod-product-compliance
Lightning Source LLC
Chambersburg PA
CBHW071742120626
46550CB00002B/621